THE TIMES

getting a **TOP JOB** as a

...PERSONAL ASSISTANT

sally longson

In this book, the feminine pronoun has been used to refer to personal assistants and the masculine pronoun to refer to their 'bosses'. This stems from a desire to avoid ugly and cumbersome language, and no discrimination, prejudice or bias is intended.

First published in 2002

Kogan Page Limited
120 Pentonville Road
London N1 9JN

The views expressed in this book are those of the author, and are not necessarily the same as those of Times Newspapers Ltd.

British Library Cataloguing in Publication Data

A CIP record for this book is available from the British Library.

ISBN 0 7494 3779 0

Typeset by Saxon Graphics Ltd, Derby

Contents

Preface

These are exciting times for anybody – male or female – seeking to acquire a role as a really good personal assistant, more commonly known as a PA. Bright, intelligent and proactive PAs are in demand. Increasingly, they are making business decisions that will affect their company. Most have close contact with clients, both internal and external, so a professional, can-do approach is essential. Some have a tremendous amount of autonomy, as they are the only linchpin in the organisation that holds the thing together.

Experience counts for much in the world of the PA, even if you've just done some temping in the holidays. This career is self-led and self-determined, perhaps more so than most. You can enhance your ability to get to the top by training to keep up to date with new technologies and skills; networking with others in your sector; raising your profile; and being very good at what you do.

Think about what's important to you

In the new millennium, we are increasingly taking on board the fact that everybody has his or her own idea of success. The old-fashioned meanings of success – money, nice house, status, a place in the community – still exist, but have been added to by spiritual virtues, such as giving something back to the community, making a difference, being happy in life, having a good balance between work and life, having the energy to do what you want to do at the end of the day instead of collapsing in front of the television. PA work offers something for everybody, whatever their own view of success is. The responsibility to make your career and role everything you want it to be rests on your shoulders. You have to make it happen because you, more than anybody, know what you want out of a job and where it fits in to the rest of your life. (There are some things it's better for the boss *not* to know.) Aside from the financial benefits and perks, PA work brings with it enormous flexibility in terms of when and where you work, and enhances your ability to pick up work practically anywhere in the job market.

Looking ahead

Tell relatives that you're going to be a secretary, and they will immediately assume you're going to type letters all day. Tell them you're thinking of being a PA, and they'll have even less idea of what you'll be doing. Most families and friends have little idea of what people do all day, which is a pity because work is important to people – it defines who they are. The Information Age, dominated by desktop and laptop computers, e-mail and the Internet, has changed a secretary's role beyond recognition. Don't let the labels 'administration' and 'support' careers, or relatives who think you'll be consigned to a life in the typing pool, put you off investigating it further. PA work is much more exciting than that. The more you go out of your box, the more exciting and rewarding the job will be, because you'll probably be doing things you want to do.

Another traditional and now outdated view of the PA role is that it is for women only. While the majority of PAs are women, increasing numbers of positions are being taken on by men. The demand made on PAs to use managerial and administrative skills every day has encouraged men to take on PA roles, particularly where these roles are combined with project management skills such as information technology. The greater emphasis on transferable skills and technical abilities has reduced the elements of the role women were traditionally perceived to be adept at, such as shorthand, typing and tea-making. As a result, men are putting a toe into the waters of the PA world and finding a niche.

This book seeks to broaden your knowledge and understanding of support roles and the route to working with these major achievers, and to help you find your niche among the huge range of opportunities secretarial work, in its very broadest terms, has available so that you can locate the 'top job' for you with an eye on excelling in your fields.

Chapter 1 looks at how things have changed in the PA/secretarial world. It's important that you know that, because the changes in management structures and information technology have transformed the role of PA from one of second-in-command and general secretary–typist–tea-maker, to partner in many companies. Chapter 2 looks at the position of PAs within companies and helps you ascertain how much of a meaty role you want. Chapters 3 and 4 introduce the skills top PAs need to do an effective job; but they also help you focus on the skills you want to use on the job, which will give it the emphasis you want. They consider the different sectors and organisations PAs can work for, and help you work out which qualities you want to use on the job and find a role in an area that you care about. Chapter 5 considers your choices in terms of how and where you work, how to give your career an international flavour if you so desire or that entry into running your own business. Chapter 6 looks at the skills and qualities you'll need and the qualifications you can get to kick off your career. The skills required to be a top PA are constantly upgrading, as PAs take on more responsibilities and enjoy greater autonomy in their work – but you have to choose the right role. Chapter 7 turns to the places you can search to find that perfect job for you, while Chapter 8 gives hints on applying for roles and ensuring you're not going to get stuck in a role that is pure remedial work. The two final chapters, 9 and 10, are designed to help you excel in your role and to manage your career so that you steer it in the direction you want.

It's your career – so drive it

This book will have plenty of tips scattered through it to help you find the niche for you. As a PA, you can put yourself at the forefront of change and in the driving seat, pushing back your boundaries of skill, and up your confidence, by doing and making things happen. Stick to the rules and your job description, and you'll be the traditional secretary. Break them in the good name of benefiting your employer, and you'll go places and feel far greater freedom as you mould the role to your own. A role is what you make of it; and this book will help you create a top job out of any PA position, even if you're in one now. Every job has something you don't like doing. The key to a top job is finding something that means something to you – and one in which the 'don't like' factor is absolutely minimal.

1

From typist and tea-maker to decision maker and taker – what's changed in the secretarial world

PAs have been empowered by a changing world

How times have changed! Traditional secretaries typed letters, did the filing and made the tea. Their working day consisted of doing routine, mundane jobs and they weren't expected to be decision makers and takers. Today, thanks to the communications and information technology revolution, and dramatic changes to management structures, in many organisations the traditional secretary has become the thoroughly modern PA. And in others, that evolution is well under way.

Of course, there are firms that still want to keep the secretary confined to the limits of the job description, and there are secretaries who are happy to take such roles. But overall, surveys undertaken by recruitment agencies show that more PAs are doing tasks previously allocated to junior and middle managers such as organising conferences, handling recruitment and preparing and delivering presentations, and managing car fleets. As layers of management were stripped away and the trend of empowering employees to make decisions and take responsibility took hold, PAs seized their moment and used the opportunity to take some of their responsibilities on instead. As a result, they frequently make decisions that impact closely on the running of an organisation, especially in smaller companies. And now, increasing numbers of PAs have degrees and are recruited for their intelligence and interpersonal skills, and their ability to hit the ground running. They have excellent communication, management and information technology skills, and the ability to multi-task at high speed. PAs manage and organise people, events, resources, information and projects in every sector. They are the organisers, trainers and supervisors within organisations whom people automatically turn to, the people who are known to keep a cool head in a crisis. The level of skill required to be a top PA will continue to rise, and PAs will have to respond to this challenge and be more highly competent than ever before, if they are to continue their enjoyed success and status. So what factors have driven this change?

Top PAs need outstanding communication skills – they work more closely with people than ever before

PAs hold businesses, teams and the lives of high-flyers and entrepreneurs together. They act as a linchpin, pulling people at all levels together to work on projects, and facilitating the smooth flow of information, discussion and ideas across people. They are the ambassadors who greet clients and customers, so the way PAs portray themselves in terms of appearance, behaviour and vocals is all-important. They organise business meetings on the other side of the world, and some travel with their bosses to take notes and see that everything runs smoothly.

The ability to handle and manage people at every level is a key element in the success of PAs – no longer can they hide behind a typewriter. PAs who can bring ideas, initiative, personality and energy to a role are in demand. Emotional intelligence is a key requirement, giving PAs a social deftness that enables them to empathise with people at any level and under any circumstance. They are in a position to learn a great deal about people – what makes them tick, what motivates them, how different individuals have their own special talents and values. In the old days, typing letters and filing didn't require this sort of skill.

As a PA, you really can find a niche role in which you can make an impact

PAs organise the lives of teams of high-powered executives and entrepreneurs – 'I run the boss's life and make sure that everything runs like clockwork, from 6.30 am to the time he gets home – however late that is!' They see that things get done behind the scenes to make everything in the office – HQ – run smoothly. They hold the fort and run the office when their bosses are out of town. Sharp PAs are a central focal point, yet they also have the tact and diplomacy and the patience to help the boss do the most basic tasks, like finding his pencil when he is under pressure.

Trust is a key element to any successful relationships between PAs and those they work with. PAs need to earn the trust and respect of those they work for. At a senior level, they have access to highly confidential internal information, pertaining to issues such as compensation, reviews and ideas for new management structures, and data relating to their organisation's clients and customers. They act as a vital sounding board for bosses about to present new ideas to the staff, and they give feedback on prospective changes and presenting technique and style. Top PAs listen to their bosses letting off steam in the privacy of their offices, but keep the event to themselves afterwards. They cope with their bosses' changes of moods during the day without a word. They know when to keep quiet. Discretion is paramount.

We live in a knowledge-based society

The more PAs know about the sector they work in and commerce, their organisation and how it works, the more they will feel a part of it and contribute to it. PA roles offer a tremendous insight into the way a company operates. PAs are in a better position than anybody to suggest improvements and initiatives that will make a difference. Top PAs actively find out how the organisation works and who is responsible for what, and they introduce themselves to

3

other colleagues. They develop a strong network of contacts who can help them, inside the company and outside it.

Knowledge matters, but, in true *Yes, Minister* style, there are things the boss doesn't need to know. Top PAs exert the most tremendous amount of control as gatekeepers and disseminators of information. They take away all the trivia in bosses' lives, enabling bosses to focus on the essential bits, making money and bringing in new business. Top PAs actively seek to take responsibility from bosses and undertake projects themselves.

An effective PA can suggest and implement change *and* react to it

The ability to cope with change is far more important than it used to be. When secretaries just typed all day long, they could be fairly oblivious to change. Today, it's impossible to escape it, and the effective PA seeks to embrace and promote it. She needs to adapt to changing technology and systems, keep up to date with new innovations and business services designed to save people time and money. She needs to be aware of new management structures, as companies strive to make their resources meet the demands of the business world. She needs the political acumen to assess how such change will affect her role (and that of her boss and team), affording her new opportunities to move her career forward, perhaps by taking on new responsibilities or moving into a new role altogether; or by posing threats to her position. Change is all around us, and customers change in their demands and expectations, so organisations must move with them. Top PAs play a key part in delivering the message of change and selling its importance to other staff within the organisation. They are important mentors and management allies in persuading others that change is important and ensuring they have the necessary skills to understand and come through the process.

Top PAs must also react to changes in their boss's day. One phone call can change everything at a ring. PAs have to handle changes to travel itineraries and meeting plans, using electronic means to help them. Interruptions resulting in total changes to the day should be expected, especially in fast-moving corporate environments where the client comes first, first and first.

PAs want roles they can get their teeth into; they want to develop their careers

Many individuals now want to develop their careers in a way they never did before. They know they have the ability and opportunity to reach their potential. Career development loans and a plethora of learning methods enable people to study for a new career or job-related qualifications at any time and place, whatever their financial status and whatever the boss says. In the past, it was harder to retrain for a new career or to reach one's potential: you stuck to what you had. Today, people are more inclined to seek variety, choice and a challenge within their work, because those are within reach. People want to feel as though they've made a difference and that their efforts have been recognised. Top PAs have a wealth of experience of business, its peaks and troughs, of handling people and in making things happen and knowing how organisations work. Businesses are waking up to that, and using that resource. And PAs are networking as professionals in their own right and learning from each other.

Manual typist to computer whizz

In the old days, typing was a very time-consuming process, because you had to rub out errors and because of the copious amounts of repetitious typing you had to do. No wonder, then, with the arrival of the computer and wonderful short cuts such as copy and paste, and e-mail, that secretaries' lives have changed for the better. In the old days, typing was the secretaries' province – nobody else could do it. Today, thanks to developments in information technology, even CEOs and chairmen can type their own e-mails (albeit with two fingers), so PAs are free to do other things. In fact, the more PAs act as coaches, teaching bosses how to use IT, the more they will be freed up.

'Why has technology changed things so much?'

So if everybody can now type, how did secretaries survive the information technology revolution? An old argument was that many bosses like the kudos of having an assistant or secretary. But as organisations cut costs at every corner to compete, that argument alone didn't justify bosses having a secretary. For one thing, many bosses now share their PA. And far from getting rid of PAs, the fields of information tehnology and e-commerce need PAs themselves.

The fact is that IT cannot replace the personal and communicative nature of many tasks PAs now do. All the technology available hasn't lessened the need for people who can organise and support professionals, from the one-person outfits, such as a life coach or financial adviser, to the huge corporates. Professionals world-wide need people to keep them to time and ensure their day runs smoothly, and to keep the office functioning so that they can focus on the business. So immersed are they in their conference call with clients and colleagues that they don't notice it's time for their next meeting or to leave for the airport to catch that flight. Somebody with a strong personality, who won't take no for an answer from very experienced and focused, successful and respected figures, has to tell them to get a move on. And there's another factor.

PAs have had no choice but to evolve and adapt to new technology and management structures and to develop their roles, otherwise they would never have survived. They have embraced all the technological and communications developments that help them do their job more cheaply and faster than ever before. At the same time, PAs have taken on management responsibilities as layers of managers have been removed. They've worked hard to carve out new roles and cut new career paths for themselves. They work long hours and have been rewarded for their dedication by heading on up into the ranks of management. They are studying for professional examinations, networking, leading internal groups, managing projects and juggling tremendous responsibilities. And many bosses now refer to their PA as their partner, showing how much they value them.

Case study: Information demands intelligent handling
Nikki, a PA in IT

The paper-free office is still a long way off, but there's no doubt that IT has transformed the way we do business and work. Electronic diary and mailing systems and the World Wide Web were supposed to help move the day along far faster. But when bosses are faced with an in-box containing 200 or so messages first thing in the morning, they can waste an awful lot of time sifting through the rubbish to find the really crucial ones he needs to take action on. A bright PA will go through the e-mails for him before he logs on, before he even gets to the office, filing away some, deleting others. She'll do as many as she can, leaving the ones for the boss to sort out and handle as he sees fit, such as the one from a friend suggesting a round of golf on Sunday, or a funny from a friend. (It's no good being closed-minded if you're going to work in this sort of role. The bosses send the most politically incorrect e-mails of all.) By the time I've been through my boss's e-mails, there are very few left for him to handle. I print off anything he can read without worrying about someone looking over his shoulder on an aircraft – press releases, articles from the papers, that sort of thing. He catches up on his reading when he's travelling.

You also have to know how to handle confidential e-mails, even from the point of ensuring that your computer is inaccessible if you go to get a coffee or grab a sandwich. It's no good leaving it up and running if anybody can just walk past and get access to the information on there.

I can watch my boss put an entry into the electronic calendar on his laptop in our Vancouver office, while I'm in London. Suddenly, a day that was free from meetings is full. When he puts something in the calendar, if there's anything he particularly needs me to do for that meeting, then he puts it in the notes section. I can open them and start to organise or research what's needed myself, or delegate the task to somebody else, usually a business associate. I try to keep track of what needs to be done and check back with people to make sure that they are on track to get things done in time. You have to be good at delegating in this job.

I think PAs have had to become experts in IT because most bosses haven't got time to keep up to date with IT themselves. If they don't know how to do something, the PA who is a shout away is the obvious person to help out, especially if there's highly confidential information on the system. PAs are usually far better at IT than bosses – we use a wider variety of applications every day. If you can learn to short-cut your way around your PC and the Internet, you'll get far more done in your day.

The bad news about IT is that PCs and laptops raise tempers and blood pressure levels when they don't work. If you're going to be a PA, you need to be an IT trouble-shooter, which as much as anything else means keeping a calm head and temper while all around you are losing theirs.

Accountability and urgency mean every minute counts

Not only do PAs need strong computer skills, but they need to know how to think rapidly and make IT work for them as individuals and for the business. The ability to juggle several things at once is essential for top PAs. 'A sense of urgency'; 'being able to think and act fast'; 'the ability to perform in a highly professional fast-moving environment'; 'able to work well under pressure'; 'able to multi-skill': many adverts describe these as key abilities that PAs must have. Fast brains make a huge difference in a world where one telephone call changes everything. People expect a much faster turnaround time in response to their requests for information, help or action. Systems give us a great deal of intelligence: they tell us if somebody has read our e-mail or received our fax, or a package been delivered by courier. They tell us that we can expect a response. If your boss cannot respond, somebody else needs to. It's bad for client relationships if mail is left unacknowledged.

The urgency of business life today is one of the reasons why there's a call for sharp, bright, quick-thinking PAs who can cope with changing situations and demanding people. Carefully laid plans for the day can be blown in an instant, thanks to a call, e-mail or fax. The technology is there to make things happen fast, and all it needs is somebody – usually the PA – to put that technology into action, pull teams together and tell people what is going on. The speed with which you can set up a conference call with people across the globe and pass out the dial-in details is incredible. Within minutes of organising a call, you can have people in Australia, London, Dubai and New York all talking together on the phone. So PAs must be flexible, as changes to the day and to the boss's priorities and their own will happen all the time.

Men do it too

Senior PAs are taking on management responsibilities, delegating tasks, motivating others and getting results from teams of people. In 2000, according to the Equal Opportunities Commission, 67 per cent of managers and administrators were men, 33 per cent were women. Of the clerical and secretarial workers, 26 per cent were men and 74 per cent were women. As the role of the PA has become more one of a manager and administrator and less one of a secretary, and increasing numbers of middle and junior managers are displaced, men are less likely to dismiss the idea of becoming a PA. The title may change to something involving 'project manager', to give less of a female image to it.

Men are not new to this sort of role. In early times, families of great wealth and power had secretaries – confidants and trusted men who would handle all their private matters, especially affairs of state. After the Renaissance, men dominated clerical and secretarial roles, maintaining books and taking letters down. As world trade expanded, secretaries held increasingly prominent positions; and the invention of the typewriter and telephone saw women becoming firmly established as secretarial workers in the 20th century.

As the PA position demands skills that are those of managers, more men are coming back into the PA field. In 1996, women made up just over three-quarters of the total clerical and secretarial workforce. Today, agencies have noticed an increase in the number of male candidates for PA positions. Employers place greater emphasis on recruiting people who will 'fit' into a team, rather than on their sex. At the end of the day, it's teamwork and chemistry between you and your bosses, and what you can achieve and produce at work that count. The workplace has become more results-focused for every employee, with a strong emphasis on what your skills are producing and what you are contributing to the organisation.

What is important to you in life?

This book will help you consider what you want to achieve as a PA and then go out and get it. Most of us have to work to earn money so that we can live in a style we choose. Yet many lottery winners continue to work after they've hit the jackpot. What is it that drives people to continue working? The challenge and responsibility, or the importance of feeling needed, or the social life? The joy of the PA world in its broadest sense is that there is something for everyone, whatever your individual goals.

Getting a top job means different things to individuals. Some people work as PAs because they recognise that it is possible to have a challenging and responsible job but have a life as well. They see professionals working all hours, being on call and cancelling holidays at the last minute and decide it's not for them. Of course, if you want a job with lots of responsibility and autonomy, you'll need the stamina and energy for long hours; your professionalism won't allow you to push off to the pub when you know something urgent needs to be done. But as the workplace has become more relaxed and dynamic, it is easier to become more involved in what is going on, and it's more important to be passionate about it. And top PAs are carving out a niche for themselves that encompasses the right amount of responsibility and autonomy and creativity for them. If their current employer won't enable them to do this, they are moving on to one that will.

As careers and lifestyles are intrinsically linked, it is important to work out what success means to you and plot your path to go out and get it. For some people, having a top job as a PA means they can leave the office at 5 o'clock promptly every day. Others relish the chance to be pushed to the max, with frenetic long hours, plenty of adrenalin and pressure. Consider what's important to you in a role, now and in the future, and you're more likely to land the job you want:

▨ How hungry are you to make a difference and contribute to a team goal and an organisation?
▨ How hungry are you to reach the top of your ladder? Have you got the will and drive, focus and energy, to make a sustainable effort to get there?
▨ Are you seeking to use secretarial work as an entry to a career, or in its own right, such as financial services, media or public relations?
▨ What do you want to achieve? What skills and resources will you need to get there?

The importance of good PAs cannot be overestimated

You realise how important secretaries are when you look at the salaries and package awaiting the best: £35,000 to £45,000-plus is not uncommon in London; a really hot PA in the Home Counties can pick up anywhere from £25,000 to £30,000; team secretaries are being paid around £22,000 in the City, and they tend to be at the lower levels in the structure of organisations. Taking all the additional perks into account, your salary could rival that of managers and professionals in other sectors. Obviously, pay depends on where you work and the sector you work in, but compare the salaries top PAs make to those of professionals in other sectors. You'll realise how much they are worth. Take a look at *Crème* in *The Times* (a weekly Wednesday supplement for PAs and secretaries) and look at the salaries on offer. You'll see what I mean. You'll also get an idea for how much pay differs between sectors.

Attitude counts

Like everything in life, your attitude will make or break your career. Top PAs are empowered individuals who want to go in and make a real difference and an impact. PAs have more chance than ever before to put their own personal stamp on a role. They have moved from a position of subordinate to partner as layers of management have been removed. Developments in the IT arena have afforded them the time and the opportunity to do other things. In short, there are far more rewards for the go-getter, in terms of job satisfaction and team effort.

As a PA, you have a responsibility to develop your own role. If your organisation won't give you the responsibility and challenges you're hungry for, find another one that will. PAs, perhaps more than any other careerists, have a chance to build on experience, adding new blocks of skills as they see fit and opportunities allow. Increasing numbers are using their skills and willingness to work hard to move into management roles or run their own business. It's up to you to take the initiative and develop your career into areas that interest you. You can make *every* job your top job if you build on your experience and develop your skills. Each new role – and organisation – will teach you something new.

Case study: Ambition makes a difference
Cathy, PA in public relations

The more involved you are in your job and the company you work in, the more passionate you feel about it and the more you give to it. It makes me sad that, for every PA who really takes the chance to make a role her own, there'll be another one who spends the day surfing the Internet for a good holiday, reading magazines, organising her social life and gossiping to friends because the job is 'boring'. Well, the world doesn't owe you a living. If you're bored at work, it's up to you to do something about it, instead of whingeing on about it all the time.

We all spend too much time at work to be unhappy there. Find a role that means something to you and excites you, or create a top job out of it. This book will help you do just that.

Summary

To get _your_ top job, you need:

- self-knowledge (so that you know exactly what you want, not just in a job but in your life as well);
- an awareness of the opportunities available and how to secure the right one for you (eg how to write a CV, hunt for the right job, network);
- chemistry with the people you work for – if you're going to work long hours together, you need to be able to hit it off and form a tight-knit team;
- the right approach and attitude: proactive, professional, committed to getting things right first time, stamina, commitment;
- the willingness to push back boundaries and expand your role through your own efforts and initiative;
- the opportunity and drive to shape the role and make it your own, by stamping your creativity and personality, initiative and emotional intelligence on it.

2

What's in a name? Peel off the title; go to the heart of the job

The role of a PA is based on a number of criteria, such as the way an organisation is structured; how it views its PAs and makes use of their talents; how individual bosses view the PA role and what sort of working relationship they expect to have with them; and what PAs themselves want from a role and how far they seek to make it their own.

To understand what a top job means to you, you need to have a broad picture of the world of work, and how sectors, organisations and teams work together. You need to understand what organisations want to achieve and to know what drives the people who work for them. You'll need to work out what you want from the workplace. Try to build up a picture of the workplace, best done by getting out there and making the most of any experience you can acquire. Reflect on what you've seen and learn from it. Talk to people in work and find out what they do and think about the workplace, and where they fit. Listen to what they're saying and, if you think 'I could do that' or 'That sounds like me!', find out more.

Where does a PA fit in the workplace?

Organisations wouldn't be able to function without the employees in support roles who ensure that the detail gets seen to. The bosses may bring in the business and look after the overall big picture and their company's mission and goals, but the support staff are the very foundations upon which they rely to keep the organisation functioning. At the end of the day, bills still need to be paid, invoices sent out, IT systems maintained, presentations created and clients greeted by a human voice when the boss is out of the office. Without such support, organisations would collapse. So who provides the support and where does the PA fit into the organisation?

Support staff cover a range of positions in the private and public sectors. Generally, the larger the organisation, the more extensive a support network there will be. The smaller the company, the more everybody will have to muck in and help out with menial tasks.

Support staff may include:

- bilingual PAs;
- board-level PAs;
- catering staff;
- executive assistants;
- farm secretaries;
- float secretaries;
- proofreaders;
- finance officers;
- word-processing operators;
- events organisers;
- evening secretaries;
- IT administrators/help desk staff;
- legal secretaries;
- marketing assistants;
- medical secretaries;
- administrators;
- office juniors;
- office managers;
- photocopying staff;
- researchers;
- receptionists;
- PAs to chief executive;
- senior PAs;
- trading floor assistants;
- telephonists;
- mail room assistants.

Many roles within the support arena offer a career ladder of their own, with their own professional organisations. But this book seeks to focus on PAs who act as the link between boss, clients and customers, and those who provide support services. PAs are like project managers who pull everybody together to get things done and ensure everything runs like clockwork behind the scenes for their internal and external clients. The standard PAs set is an important one.

Case study: PAs set the standard
Amanda, PA in insurance

I think an important part of our job is to give feedback to those who provide services and goods to their organisation, so that standards are kept up and, if possible, improved. If you're going to get things right first time and every time, you have to make sure that everybody has the information they need to do their jobs well in a language and tone that's appropriate. The way you do this shows the sort of standard of work you expect. If the PA is sloppy on the job, why should she expect any better of those whose services she uses? Top PAs must be sticklers for high standards all the time: when things don't get done as they should, PAs have to deal with it fairly and tactfully but firmly. If I find an error, I say so. It's my problem if I don't put it right. You have to be prepared to chase when things don't get done as fast as they should.

Figure 2.1 shows how the PA links everybody together to make things happen.

You'll see that PAs have to deal with a wide variety of people. Remember that, for every possible person or business a PA communicates with, each will also have their PAs/secretaries with whom the PA will form a relationship.

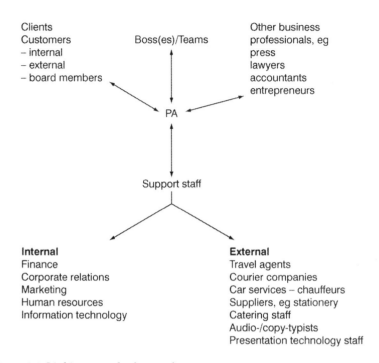

Clients
Customers
– internal
– external
– board members

Boss(es)/Teams

Other business
professionals, eg
press
lawyers
accountants
entrepreneurs

PA

Support staff

Internal
Finance
Corporate relations
Marketing
Human resources
Information technology

External
Travel agents
Courier companies
Car services – chauffeurs
Suppliers, eg stationery
Catering staff
Audio-/copy-typists
Presentation technology staff

Figure 2.1 Linking everybody together

How do support roles differ?

PAs are also known as secretaries, senior secretaries, executive secretaries, executive assistants and office managers. Some companies have a vague idea of the sort of person they want to recruit; they know they need some help, but they're not really sure what and, in reality, they mean everything. In some cases, a PA is all things to all people: secretary, receptionist, administrator, manager, trainer, events organiser... Some PAs choose their own title, depending on what they believe best reflects the job they do. Some prefer to be called a senior secretary, others a senior PA. Both may have similar jobs. The bottom line is that PAs must be versatile and adaptable people, able and willing to turn their hands to practically anything to meet the needs of the business and the demands of clients, even if it means going against their own personal beliefs. The work is never clearly defined – it can include anything and everything. This is not unusual in the work-place – most job descriptions go past their sell-by date rapidly.

Since there are a great number of support roles, it will help if you can identify your own particular talents, aspirations and moti-vations. You can then discriminate in your own mind how the role you want will differ from others in the secretarial arena, and determine how much responsibility and autonomy you want.

To give you an idea of how roles differ within the PA/secretarial arena, here are some general and brief guidelines outlining what they might consist of and how much impact each can make. Read through them and decide which appeal to you and why. Remember, these are only guidelines – a PA in one firm may do some of the work of an office manager in another.

Office manager

The office manager oversees the smooth day-to-day running of the office by:

- recruiting staff such as secretaries and administrators, recep-tionists and temps, office services staff;
- selecting suppliers of stationery, office equipment, couriers, travel agencies, recruitment agencies;
- ensuring that office equipment functions smoothly, such as telephones, fax machines, computers;
- maintaining computer records, including perhaps staff records of absence, holidays, sick leave, starting and finishing dates;
- outlining the structure of the support staff;
- applying health and safety regulations;
- ensuring budgets are met and preparing monthly reports of expenses and financial summaries;
- organising internal meetings and social events;
- improving office systems.

Some office managers delegate some of their responsibilities to PAs who want to take on extra tasks to boost their own skills. In smaller companies, the role of PA and office manager may belong to the same person. Office managers need a thorough understanding of how an office and people work, and strong communications and computing skills. They must be able to see the bigger picture, while paying attention to detail, and be able to pick up technology fast and handle several things at once. They also need to be fit and first-class troubleshooters.

Personal assistant

The personal assistant supports a team or individual by:

- working closely at senior level with key people internally and externally;
- doing research on the Internet and preparing presentations;
- managing a very busy diary, which may include personal events in the boss's life;
- organising meetings and travel itineraries;
- liaising with clients and colleagues by phone, fax, e-mail and in person;
- handling and creating correspondence, some of which will be of a highly confidential nature;
- carrying out _ad hoc_ projects as determined by the PA and/or boss, which may be determined by the boss's role within the organisation and the sector.

Within organisations, there has been a shift from the PA working for one boss towards the _team secretary_ providing support for a group of people, even at a senior level, or the PA working for one or two people, but taking on additional responsibilities, as an _independent secretary_. The Institute of Employment Studies identified these two new secretarial roles as early as 1996. Those working for one person within an organisation are likely to do so only at the most senior level, where some chief executives may have two PAs: a senior one and a junior assistant. That said, there are still opportunities for PAs to work for one-person outfits, such as entrepreneurs or celebrities – writers, chefs, fitness gurus or academics. Many entrepreneurs and famous people have their own PAs, on whom they are totally dependent. They may be wacky whirlwinds, rarely in the office, usually travelling on the road, doing what they love, full of life and energy, and totally dependent on the PA to plan their lives and hold the fort. It requires a particular energy to be a PA to work with these dynamic people, plus tremendous independence and resourcefulness, as you'll be working on your own. These individuals have driven themselves hard to get to where they are, and are hungry for success and to see that things are just right. They can be frustrating to work for, but, when they are at the top of their professions, you also get a particular kick out of working for people who are respected in and out of their sector for what they have achieved.

PAs must be able to multi-task and thrive on being busy. As they have lots of client contact, they need to be able to put the client first, which may mean staying late frequently to get things done. They may also have particular responsibilities that are reflected by the boss's position within the organisation. For example, chairmen and CEOs of huge corporates have particularly broad briefs, as this advertisement shows: 'A highly competent PA is required by the Chairman who has world-wide business, academic, charitable and private interests. The role is exceptionally demanding, comprising a variety of activities including personal and family matters.'

Case study: The serious, professional approach is essential

Angela, works for the chairman of a bank

CEOs and chairmen need someone who will handle personal, business and charity work to a very high standard. If you're going to work for people at the top of huge corporates, it's important to remember that they may be members of industry groups, committees and forums, with business interests such as franchising and education–industry partnerships. They'll visit other countries, either to other offices or to meet and do business with other clients, perhaps to sit on committees which discuss global issues for the company. They'll have personal interests – often hunting, fishing, shooting, golf – which mean they can network. They're going to be very high-profile. You have to be used to dealing with very senior people outside the company and yet be aware of the total sphere of their management responsibilities within it. They'll impact on huge numbers of people if you're working for a large global company. They need the overall picture of what's happening in their sector and organisation, yet to retain an eye for detail at the same time.

I think it's really important that I portray the right image on their behalf. Everything has to run very smoothly – there's no room for mistakes at the top. You have to be very professional, and demand very high standards from everybody else you come into contact with – you can't allow them to get away with anything sloppy. Everything must run smoothly and this can mean attending to any details at all which get in the way of such a process. You have to correct anything which isn't right by calling in the right people to sort it out.

These are the people who probably fly first class across the Atlantic, have country homes and ones in London, accounts with private banks, their kids go to private schools... You might handle family matters, such as booking the family holiday, collecting tax information, handling the school fees, house and car insurance, and social events.

At this level, you need extensive experience and an enquiring mind. You need to be totally committed to the job. You'll cope with eager clients who think they've got an exclusive right to your boss, and pushy subordinates all keen to get their time with the boss. As his right hand, you need to know what needs to be done in the boss's day. My hours are very long – I start at 8.30 and never leave until about 7.30 or 8 at night, but I go home feeling as though I've been challenged in doing the best job I can for a guy who appreciates what I do.

Combining roles

Some organisations (especially small ones) combine roles right from the start.

Case study: Combining roles

Nigella, office manager/PA, mining company

I look after the managing director 30 per cent of my time, and oversee all aspects of running the building for 70 per cent of it. Without me, half the things which need to get done wouldn't. My boss rarely says to me, 'Can you do this?', because he is so focused on the business that he doesn't even know the routine tasks which need doing. In the last year, I've negotiated a lot with suppliers, which has toughened me up a lot, especially when the cleaning staff started to slack off and I had to arrange a meeting with their boss to talk about it. I told my boss what was going on, and explained what I proposed to do about it, and he was very supportive and made a couple of suggestions about ways I could approach the issue, but basically it was down to me. It was my problem and I had to solve it fast; if I hadn't, what sort of message would that have given everybody in the company about the standards I expected?

You never know what's going to come your way and you just have to be prepared for anything and able to think fast on your feet. It's one of the challenging things about PA work – two days are never the same. Last week, we had an unexpected call from the Russian embassy to say they had people in London who wanted to meet my boss for lunch the following day. I had to find a venue with suitable menu, and find someone who would translate menus and do name cards and table cards within 24 hours and deliver them to the hotel. I also managed to brief my boss on each of the visitors as well, and what was going on in Russia, in terms of politics and business, so he would be well prepared. It's that never knowing what's going to happen that makes it such a challenge. You just have to be totally unflappable and think fast on your feet.

Some PAs work for a couple of people but also have their own projects and responsibilities in their own right. These may focus on areas such as IT or human resources, or marketing and business development.

Case study: Personal responsibilities

Sarah, PA to two directors, international recruitment company

One of my responsibilities is to organise the weekly internal meeting which takes place in our European offices simultaneously, so they all know what's happening that week, and can talk about new clients and business development initiatives and anything else they need to discuss. I arrange a meeting room, and dial in numbers for those people in our European offices – Vienna, Paris, Madrid and Prague. I prepare the agenda, ensure that any speakers are ready and know where they have to be when, send out any documents people will need to read through in good time for the meeting and then ensure that any points to be actioned are followed up on. It's a tremendous responsibility, when you're dealing with highly paid professionals whose time is extremely short, to ensure that everything runs smoothly. It means I have considerable contact with the IT people, to make sure that all the videoconference systems are ready to go.

Team PA/secretary

The team PA/secretary supports a team by:

- looking after two or more people;
- doing travel itineraries;
- reimbursing expenses;
- producing presentations and formatting documents;
- answering the telephone and taking messages;
- typing documents or arranging for their typing;

▪ pulling the team together;
▪ disseminating information throughout the team.

The fun within the role of team secretary is in handling dynamic personalities who nonetheless work well together in a team environment. Some teams are very volatile and lively, where there's lots of excitement and rarely a dull moment. In other teams, nobody will like the bad-tempered and irritable boss. It's part of your role to understand those dynamics and pull the team together, and important not to take things personally. Team secretaries must be assertive, and able to manage pressure and conflicting demands.

Case study: Team secretaries need to understand team dynamics

Amanda, PA in insurance

I work for a team of four people – a managing director, marketing director, plus two associate professionals. I have to be really organised and use my judgement in terms of what is urgent or not, especially when two people come to me with something to do at once. Then you have to stop them in their tracks. It's a real juggling act to keep all four balls in the air at the same time – you have to be able to prioritise your workload, doing the time-sensitive stuff first. I always check with my team to find out whose is the most urgent at the outset, which prevents problems later on. Within many teams, there will be a ranking of seniority with a team leader or most senior person. Most people within the team will recognise that there will be times when you're stretched, but, when they all want something at once, they have to decide whose work comes first. You'll always have one or two in a team with bigger egos than the rest who think their stuff comes first. You have to have a strong personality, and not get put off by being hassled by several people at once.

Independent PAs

Some roles will be very autonomous, especially if the PA works for a one-person outfit, such as an author or celebrity, or in a very small specialist company, or holds the fort in an environment where there are no managers, such as a private club. For example, a private garage advertised for a PA with a clean driving licence and strong co-ordination skills, as the responsibilities included collection and delivery of cars, booking cars in, welcoming customers, car security on the forecourts and the ordering of valet supplies. This sort of role probably involves working a lot without any supervision, so would need a confident and sociable individual who is a first-class problem solver and troubleshooter. Some private families have PAs to run their households and lives.

Case study: If you're going to work on your own, you must be resourceful

Pat, works for a family in Chelsea

Basically, I run the household. I recruit staff like the cooks, gardeners and butler. I liaise with them constantly about social events I have to organise so that they know what to prepare and how many people to expect and can make sure they have what they need. I have an annual budget to run the house. If there's a special event coming up, then I have an extra sum of money to plan for it. This year, Sasha will be 18, so she and I are having fun planning her birthday party, which will be held in June, in the family's country home in Sussex. I oversee the practical running of the house, calling in electricians and plumbers if anything goes wrong. I check all the insurance is up to date and organise the family holidays. It's very demanding and the hours are long, but I'm well paid for it. I went to the States last year with the family, as they wanted to buy a property in Florida, and it was my job to liaise with agencies over there so we had some properties to look at when we arrived.

You must be very resourceful, and able to work with the minimum of supervision and maximum autonomy. Some people may miss the team spirit of offices, but then the surroundings you work in may make up for it. I network with other PAs in the same position – we meet for lunch, that sort of thing, and bounce ideas and information off each other, but we're very discreet about the families and people we look after. I think to do this job well – any PA job well – you have to have the interests of those you look after at heart. It's actually a very caring role, because you come to know your boss and their loved ones – family and friends – very well.

Secretary

The secretary supports a team or individual by undertaking secretarial and administrative tasks:

- handling correspondence and opening the mail;
- keeping records, such as holiday time;
- undertaking general office work;
- answering the telephone and taking messages;
- taking dictation by shorthand or listening to audiotapes;
- filing documents;
- making tea/coffee;
- *ad hoc* duties.

Traditional secretaries have a narrower focus and are more likely to work with the boss or team alone. They are likely to have less of an impact across the firm, to be hard-working, reliable and cheerful, and to be good team players who won't make and shake the world but won't upset people on the telephone either. Firms employing secretaries for such roles will probably want successful candidates to be in them for a while with no chance of parole.

Word processor operator/typist

The word processor operator/typist supports a team or individual (which may include PAs):

- typing and amending documents such as reports, memos, presentations and proposals, faxes and letters;
- proofreading the final product;
- attending to layout on the page to create the right image;
- typing from audiotapes or copy-typing;
- saving documents in the correct place.

There are still straightforward typing roles that exist, and you'll see them advertised: '9–5, no hassle, just straight typing for a charming boss'. Usually, bosses recruiting this sort of help are house-trained and handle their own diaries and clients (or they have somebody else such as a PA to do these tasks), but like to leave the typing to a very fast expert. So speed and accuracy are all-important, along with attention to detail, proofreading abilities and care over document layout.

Some people _do_ want a straightforward traditional support role, where they can come in to work, get on with what they have to do and then leave with no thought of the office. If that's you, why not create your own top job in such a role by building up a reputation for being the fastest and most accurate person in the building, who turns documents around faster than anybody else?

Office junior

The office junior supports a team in an office:

- distributing incoming faxes and sending out faxes;
- photocopying materials;
- booking taxis;
- arranging refreshments such as tea and coffee;
- dealing with deliveries;
- sorting the post;
- typing;
- delivering messages and parcels;
- doing a stint on reception.

The office junior post is traditionally one in which the school leaver with GCSEs (at the very least English and maths at grade C) and a year in further education will kick off his or her career. Enthusiasm and a willingness to muck in and help out others are essential qualities. Most employers expect you to know how an office functions and how to behave in a business environment. Many hope the role will act as a springboard for you to move on to bigger and better things after a year or thereabouts, so being willing and able to learn are crucial qualities. If you see the role as your step into the workplace in the PA arena, find out what happened to the last office junior, so that you have an idea of what the future holds with the company. The post of office junior offers a good way to develop an insight into how a company works and to learn a lot about business and people if you keep your eyes and ears open!

'Who determines what a role involves? How can I find out what the boss wants of an assistant?'

As I mentioned at the start of this chapter, the kind of role you're likely to end up with will depend on a number of criteria. Some bosses have a very fixed idea of what they want their PA to do and have no intention of letting you move totally out of that realm. So it's important to suss out what the past and future role could involve at interview. Chapter 8 will help you do this.

When choosing your top job, you need to consider the position you want to hold in a team, both now and in the future. Where do you want to sit in the pack? Some of us want to be central to it, so a post as a team secretary might be appropriate. Others prefer to develop their own area of work and responsibilities and be more independent, which can be lonelier but allow more autonomy.

What makes a role all you want it to be?

To find the right sort of level of job for you, that is, *your* top job, build an idea of what your day would consist of (see Figure 2.2), so that you can find a job that suits you. What does your life history say about you and the sort of person you are? Are you a leader, do

Figure 2.2 Your day

you relish and thrive on challenges or do you prefer a more peaceful life?

The level of challenges, pressure and variety you have will depend on your experience and drive. For example, the office junior may have responsibility for ensuring that the stationery cupboard is kept tidy and well stocked. The more experienced PA may be responsible for finding a supplier for the stationery cupboard who will provide the best value for money and the range of goods most appropriate to the organisation's needs. The office junior may be recruited by the PA and/or office manager. The PA has far more opportunity to impact on a business because of greater experience and skills, but the office junior can develop these and gain a thorough grounding of experience necessary to move on to greater things.

The way a role develops depends partly on your willingness to push through boundaries and take on new challenges. If you never want any real responsibility or challenges, then you don't have to volunteer for anything. The problem with this approach is that your career stands still – but the world moves on.

What does a top job mean to you?

Everybody has a different idea of what career success is. One person may take it to mean stacks of money in the bank, stocks and shares, a fabulous home and a sports car. Another may feel success is more to do with making a difference to something he or she feels strongly about – perhaps an environmental issue or child welfare. Success at work can be measured in many ways, such as:

- Recognition – 'The boss and company recognise I'm doing a good job.'
- Achievement of a specific goal – 'I write the monthly newsletter, publish it and send it out to our members.'
- Respect – 'People treat each other well at work.'
- Responsibility – 'This project is my responsibility.'
- Leadership – 'I lead a team of secretaries.'
- Power – 'I established the IT policy for the company.'
- Good salary – 'I want to save lots of money to buy my first flat.'
- Fun environment – 'I look forward to going to work: there's a great atmosphere.'
- Happiness – 'I love what I'm doing.'
- Status – 'I work for the people at the top.'
- Targets – 'I want to set up a new IT system by March.'
- A sensible balance of work and play – 'I can always leave on time.'
- To contribute to something that means a lot to you – 'I make a difference to something I really care about.'
- Enough pay so you can enjoy life – 'I want a 9 to 5 job.'
- To travel with the job – 'I go to other European offices to help with staff training.'
- To use a particular talent – 'I use my languages on the job.'
- To use the job to step on to something else – 'I want to get into financial services.'

What you consider essential to a job, somebody else won't. Some people love pressure, or relish receiving phone calls from the office over the weekend or while they're on holiday. Individuals all want different levels of responsibility, variety, pressure; you need to consider how much *you* want. Do you want to work for very senior people where life is much more serious, or for a fun and friendly team, where you can relax a bit more?

Case study: Think about what you want in life
Angela, PA to a hotel director

Think about your values in life, such as the work/play balance and the hours you work. It isn't uncommon now for top PAs to work 12-hour days. You can get a sense of the commitment demanded by a company by the conditions it places on its employees in adverts. Some jobs will demand that you have the minimum of commitments such as a partner, kids or pets. This means that you are likely to be 'on call' to go anywhere, at the employer's demand. Adverts with phrases like 'must be totally committed – this is not a 9–5 role' are telling you something. You may be excited by a salary of £35,000 a year, but think how this will relate to what you want from life. Will you have the energy and time to fit in other things which are important to you, and, importantly, can you be sure that your evening plans won't suddenly be cut short by the necessity to stay late at work? I have to say that I've always found the more involved you get in a job and the more you get to know your colleagues, the more willing you'll find yourself to spend longer at the office. But it's a consideration – you'll always get people who want to leave at bang on 5 o'clock.

My job doesn't pay as well as other sectors, but I enjoy it. I wanted something social, and I love meeting the guests and talking to them. It's useful because I get lots of feedback – the positive and the not-so-good – and I always try to pass it back to the departments. Either it makes them feel good about what they do or it tells them to push the standard up. Recently, I got fully involved in doing the refurbishment of the public rooms. My boss and I talked about the atmosphere we wanted to create, and then he left the rest to me. I chose a lot of the decor and checked that we were within our budget and the timescale we were working to. That's one of the great things for me about this job – the way I am totally involved in the running of the hotel.

It's important to put these things into perspective. You may be reading this book as you finish a course in further or higher education, or as you contemplate a career change. If this is your first full-time job out of school or further education college, you may simply be looking to land a job as your main goal, and find your feet at work as a full-time employee as a first step into the workplace. Perhaps you're looking for a company that will offer a good training scheme. If you've just graduated, you might be looking to bide some time while you decide what sort of role you want, and see temping as a good way to start paying off those student debts while you kick your career ideas around in your head; or you might be hungry for responsibility and challenges. You could also be looking for secretarial work as a route into a highly competitive area, such as media. Or you could be looking to give some oomph to your current role.

Much depends on what career success means to you. Talk to your friends about their view of success and see how it differs from yours. It's important to identify where you are now and where you want to be in the future, so that you can work out how to get there and plot your career path accordingly.

Summary

- Don't let others' perceptions of what the PA role entails put you off choosing a career in this line of work – ask yourself how much they honestly know about it.
- Know what sort of success you want at work, and then plot your path to achieve it.
- Establish long-term goals ('I want to be a top-flight PA in five years' time') and short-term goals ('I want to do a PowerPoint course in the next six months') that complement each other.
- Be sure what you're letting yourself in for when considering a position – Chapter 8 will tell you how to do this.

3 What do you particularly love doing and want to be involved in?

When you consider where your niche is in the workplace, think about your values, needs and interests, and the approach you like, and how each sector relates to them. Talk to the people in it. Would you want to work closely with them? If you're going to be with like-minded people, then you'll need to identify what your interests and values are first. You must be prepared to learn the lingo and talk the talk of the sector you work in. Some PAs will be totally committed to a particular sector; others will prefer to move from one to another. Think about the clients and customers you'll deal with on the telephone and in person; and think about the salary levels and working conditions. The next two chapters will help you work through these issues, but you'll need to do more thinking about yourself and the sort of person you are, and how you relate to the opportunities the workplace offers, to find your niche.

What makes you tick? What sort of culture do you want and where do you want to make a difference?

When thinking about where you want to work, it's important to consider what makes you tick and the sort of culture you want to work in. These issues are important, because your life as a whole will be profoundly affected by them. If you want to make big bucks, you'll need to look for the sectors that have big financial rewards such as investment banking and the legal profession. If you want to put something back into the community, you could consider the non-profit sector, and work for local government or charity, but the financial rewards won't be so hot. If a balance of life and work is crucial to you, then you're better off looking for work in the public sector, because you're more likely to leave when your contract says you will, for example at 5 o'clock. The public sector is better practised in providing flexitime, job-sharing opportunities and family-friendly perks, such as crèches. You're less likely to be discriminated against. And increasing numbers of people are turning to the public sector, anxious to do something they consider worth while, as opposed to just raking in the cash.

On the other hand, the public sector often takes far longer to recruit staff because of the process, which could take weeks; in the private sector, you could find yourself starting work within a few days. In the public sector, you may end up being a victim of verbal and physical abuse from those people you are trying to help. Talk to people working in both sectors and compare notes. It will help you work out where your niche is.

Think about the culture you prefer to work in, and which of the attributes shown in Table 3.1 appeal to you most.

As employers look for people who will be a good 'fit' into organisations, so they look for people whose values match theirs. Many organisations in the professional sector – accountancy, law, banking, management consultancy – have slightly more aggressive ambitions, such as 'Our goal is to be the number one provider of financial services in our field.' As a PA, you can contribute to the efforts of an organisation to achieve any one of these goals *and* work with people whose values mirror yours. In these environments, you need to be an achiever, someone who is committed to putting the client first, with bags of confidence, and a team player who works well with anyone, particularly cross-borders.

Table 3.1 Your preferred culture

Attributes (1)	Attributes (2)
Informal dress *Jeans and a sweatshirt will do.*	Formal business attire *A suit – with skirt or trousers – will hit the spot.*
Fast-moving and changing *Things change hour by hour.*	Relaxed *Plenty of time to have a coffee*
Fun people who think 'out of the box' *Why don't we do this like this?*	People sticking to rules and regulations *The policy is... so we can't...*
Safe *Redundancies are rare.*	Volatile *Risky in terms of job security*
Ethical *We do not work with any companies that use animals to test products.*	*What are ethics?*
Young industry *If you're over 30, you're past it.*	Caters for all ages *My grandmother works there.*
Level of pay is terrible *You're not in it for the money.*	Pay is great, but it's the bonuses that count plus share options and perks. *Of course you're in it for the cash!!! Why else would you do it?*
Out-of-the-box types *More room for individuals and creativity*	More institutionalised and corporate *You like a structured approach.*
Lunch is for friends and shopping	What's lunch?

Case study: Think about the people you're going to be working with

Susanne, PA in an investment bank

No two days are ever the same in this environment – it's really fast-paced and very aggressive. If somebody was going into investment banking, one of the key things I'd say is you need to be tough and tenacious and confident. I look after a very busy senior guy. I've always got people demanding to see him and have to be very firm when there's no space in his schedule. I spend a lot of time organising meetings, getting my boss to where he needs to be, liaising with clients and internal staff, organising complex travel itineraries. A lot of things are last-minute. Last night, at 7, I still didn't know whether Jack was going to Paris or Krakow the following morning. It's a matter of making every minute count. Since I started in this job, my technical skills and ability to turn things around have really improved. You need to be tenacious and confident; it's not suitable for people who are going to get walked all over. Investment bankers can be aggressive and very demanding in their haste to get things done. It's true what they say about the long hours – I've had many a very late night here, but the bonuses and base salary make all the difference, although they depend on how the markets are doing. You have to be able to work cross-border, with people of all over the world – we're a global organisation – who are very focused and ambitious, hard-working and driven to succeed and win. I adore it, but it's not for everyone.

Case study: I wanted a fun environment that was a bit different

Jane, works for a property company

An individual's home will be the biggest investment they make in their lives – so they are bound to want to get the niggly bits right. Sometimes, you or your boss will be telling them things they don't want to hear which concern their homes or money. You have to be adept at dealing with lots of people and working to deadlines – things can get very stressful, especially when properties are due to be exchanged or sales completed. But we all really help each other out here and, after the day is over, we all head off to the pub for a few drinks – it's very sociable; everyone goes along. It's almost expected really. One of the things I liked about the advert for the job was the opening line: 'If you believe in life after 5, then this is the job for you!'

Who do you want your clients to be?

Think about the circumstances in which you will feel happy handling your clients, and in which they will relate to your values and motivations to work, and you'll get an idea of what you're in for. Consider whom you feel most comfortable handling or have most compassion for:

- general public;
- parents;
- journalists/press;
- farmers;
- charities;
- creative people in arts, media;
- academics;
- people in trouble with the law;
- those who sell their expertise to others;
- tourists;
- customers as individuals;
- business professionals, such as lawyers or bankers;
- children;
- students;
- celebrities;
- politicians;
- engineers;
- entrepreneurs;
- chairmen;
- those who are sick;
- diplomats;
- clients;
- consultants/advisers;
- royalty.

It's important to think about who you want your clients to be, because you'll be dealing with them all day. Think about how much direct contact you want with your customers and clients. Do you want a face-to-face role, meeting and greeting people, or do you prefer to be out of sight, perhaps on the end of a telephone? Do you want to handle your customers directly, or work in a unit that works to benefit others and help them, but rarely gets to meet them? For example, if you worked in education, you could work in a school where you'd have constant contact with kids and their parents. If you didn't want regular contact with kids, but wanted to work in education, you could work for the local education authority or adult education colleges or universities. Here the atmosphere will be quite different.

Pinpoint the people you want to work with and for; then you can start identifying organisations that work with them or employ them, and you'll be able to start looking at the area you want to work in. The choice is enormous: PAs work in the private and public sectors, in government, professional organisations and charities, in small and medium-sized companies and for entrepreneurs, celebrities and large corporates.

How much responsibility and autonomy do you want?

Top PAs may find themselves managing a whole number of areas, including people (their boss and other support staff), resources, information, projects and events, as well as *ad hoc* projects such as conferences or selecting new office suppliers. The more senior you are, the more responsibility you can take on. Thus you could be running the office or enjoying responsibility for projects such as:

- planning and supervising training programmes;
- choosing the car and hotel scheme to go for;
- selecting IT systems;
- purchasing supplies and arranging for their delivery;
- choosing an agency to use for temporary staff;
- recruiting lower-level staff;

- managing hospitality budgets;
- arranging conferences and corporate events;
- giving presentations to staff;
- representing management at a meeting.

These may be mutually agreed by the boss and PA; or initiated at the PA's suggestion and be entirely new to the company; or taken from the boss to lighten his or her load, while developing the PA's skills in new areas. Some secretaries now have considerable autonomy to make decisions affecting their organisation because they've developed expertise in a particular area and carved out their own role.

Case study: Work to become an expert in your niche skill

Marge, PA and manager of secretaries in a legal firm

It's really important to think about the skills you want to use on the job, because, if you're good at them and are passionate about them, unless you do something about developing a niche and using them, you won't get far. I knew I wanted to get involved in managing a team of PAs and word processor operators, and I prepared a careful case for such a role and sold it to my two bosses. I spent time outlining how it would benefit the organisation, which they liked.

Now I help develop the human resources policy for support staff and have made links with local colleges to help us find school and college leavers as new recruits. I give talks there on behalf of our company about the workplace about twice a term to different groups of students, mostly those on business studies courses. From these efforts, we've recruited two students to join our firm in September and given them a stint on work experience so they know what they're letting themselves in for.

At the same time, many PAs report their roles still include tasks such as filing, photocopying and franking the mail, making tea and coffee, collecting dry cleaning, and preparing meeting rooms, which may mean cleaning up after the meeting before. Some don't mind, because such tasks provide a break from the computer; others resent doing them completely. Every job has tasks that you dread doing, but the aim is to reduce the time you spend on them as much as possible. Which level of responsibility appeals to you? How hungry are you for something you can really get your teeth into? Although you can aim high, a flexible approach is a must because, at the end of the day, you can be asked to do anything.

What sort of pressure do you like and how fast-paced do you want your day to be?

How fast and pressured do you want work to be and how often? Organisations are far more dynamic and fast-paced than they used to be – but because you're working with a like-minded team of people, with whom you fit in well, it's more fun too. You have to think on your feet much faster, which makes life much more interesting. Some bosses and teams are busier than others at peak times of the year – are you a peak person, or do you like to have it fast and constant? The role of PA, whether you're working for a team of 4, 6 or 10, or for a couple of senior people or for one, can be a very demanding one and an amazing juggling act, which means you have to handle fast-paced environments while remaining calm throughout. Consider which sort of pressure appeals to you:

▫ Do you enjoy the sort of mornings where you barely have time to go to the loo?
▫ How do you feel about having to cancel lunch with a friend right at the last minute because of work?
▫ Lunch is for wimps.
▫ You are pressured all the time, from the minute you step in the door to the time you leave; or not at all pressured; or sometimes pressured.

▓ You work in a volatile office where anything can happen and probably will.
▓ You're on 24-hour call at peak periods.
▓ You're constantly meeting deadlines through the day and week.
▓ You set your own deadlines.
▓ You know you can make social engagements – at lunch, in the evenings – without the risk of having to cancel them because of worries about work.

People get stressed about different things, and the people working in the sector you choose to work in will have to deal with those stresses and demands. Table 3.2 gives examples of the things you'll need to handle if you work in certain sectors.

People respond to stressful situations differently. Some people handle patients on the phone, who are very ill or desperate to have a baby, with great tact and compassion; others wouldn't. Some would relish the pressure imposed on them to produce a presentation while handling other tasks at the same time; others would hate it. We all react differently and handle situations in our own way and at our own level of satisfaction. Think about the sorts of stresses and pressures you would like to handle on the job.

Table 3.2 Pressures associated with different sectors

Sector	Pressure on your client
health	people who are very anxious about the state of their health
property	clients who are trying to sell their home and move into another one within a timescale
journalism	meeting the deadline and scooping the best story
'being the global number one'	emphasis is on winning, being the best, the client or customer's first choice
recruitment	getting that next position, being headhunted, moving up the ladder, being offered a job
law	winning the case

What is important to you in an organisation?

To achieve your top job, it's important to understand what makes you tick, where you want to make a difference and what you want to achieve. When you start your job search, it will be important to look for a company that makes you think, 'I want to be a part of that organisation.' Suss out what makes that company different and why it stands from its rivals, so that you explain clearly why you want to work for it.

Most people have things that are essential to them – 'I couldn't work for a company that gave me less than five weeks' holiday a year' – and things that would be nice but aren't crucial – 'It would be nice if it had dress-down Friday, but I'm not that bothered, really.' Pinpoint your essentials and those things you're prepared to compromise over (see Table 3.3).

If you look back on your experience of the workplace to date, you'll be able to reflect on which organisations felt 'right' and those that didn't. The work chances you'll have had will have given you an idea of what sort of environments you enjoy and what you don't like or get much mileage out of. If you're thinking of a career as a PA, the probability is that you'll already have done some temping in an office or at the least done some work experience as part of a course. Look back and think of those experiences that really gave you a buzz. What did you like about them? The atmosphere, the buzz about the place, the vision and determination of the people there to do a great job? Or the fact it was so fast-paced, or so slow-paced, or that they had great coffee? Perhaps you loved the fact you were connected with a high-profile company, dealing with huge corporate clients. Maybe you preferred the organisation with a strong ethical approach, environmentally friendly, innovative, family-friendly, life-friendly, or the spirit of craziness. Do you want to work for a company that has given itself simply a local reach, or a regional or national one, or a global set-up where you'll have another dimension? Many say that the new dimension working for an international company gives you – 'It's like eating chocolate after you've tasted bread and butter' – is something you can never go back on.

Table 3.3 Pinpointing the essentials

	Essential	Nice to have	Not bothered
Good working relationship with boss/team			
Geographical location			
The journey to work			
Hours			
Opportunity to advance			
Chances to grow and develop			
Variety of work			
Salary			
Fringe benefits			
Flexitime			
Career breaks			
Family-friendly			
Atmosphere			
Reputation of firm			
Size of company			
Recognition for doing a good job			
Good social life			
Team spirit			
Ethical approach			
Non-profit			
Aggressively business-oriented			
Profile and reputation			

Some organisations like to sell themselves as sociable, fun, appealing cultures to work for and want people with a sunny disposition and a real team-player ethic. 'Must have attitude that "I work to live, not live to work."' 'A highly sociable company, so get ready for some good nights out.' 'If you are flexible, cheerful and can type at over 60 wpm, and enjoy working with creative people, call us!' 'Young, lively and dynamic environment!' 'Do you thrive in a fast-paced corporate environment?'

How large an organisation do you want to join?

The first point to stress here is not to ignore small and medium-sized companies when looking for employment, because they make an important contribution to the economy and the job market. Smaller companies can provide useful places to start off if you want to move to relevant corporates later, especially if you can't get into a particular sector. For example, if you want to work for an investment bank, working in a private equity company or financial services company will give you useful experience. Small companies should offer plenty of responsibility and variety, because there is far more emphasis on everybody mucking in and the 'all hands on deck' approach. You may also find you have more autonomy and independence, perhaps being responsible for making decisions about purchasing: stationery, courier services and travel. A smaller company is more likely to recognise effort and achievement, and could be particularly rewarding if the company is growing and expanding, giving you the chance to grow with it.

Many FTSE 100 companies look for people who've had previous experience of working for large corporates with their management structures. The CEO of a FTSE 100 company will have a very different role to that of the managing director of a company of say 40-strong. The breadth of work a PA will have to do will be quite different. In large companies, there will probably be a structure of secretaries: junior secretary, senior PA, executive PA, which means you work for increasingly senior people as you make your way up the career ladder. Initially, your role may be restricted to basics such as organising travel itineraries, doing expenses, picking up the telephone and checking e-mails. You'll need to plot your career diligently and show your ambition to work for the positions at the top, if you want to move up. In a small company, you'll be landed with lots of responsibility and variety early on simply because there's no one else to do it.

Summary

▒ When looking for a job as a PA, it's important to consider what you like doing, because the workplace is so results-focused.
▒ Think about the sort of person you are – do you like to work on your own or within a tight-knit team?
▒ Think too about what is important to you in a job – all these factors will help you define the sort of role you're looking for.

4 *Different roles demand their own skills*

Whatever they do, people at work all use transferable skills. Examples of these are communication, numeracy, information technology, team working, problem solving and working alone and unsupervised. Top PAs need to use all of these skills. They may also feel more comfortable applying these to certain situations. For example, some people will be quite at home in professional firms, such as banking, law, accounting and management consultancy. Others will prefer to work in areas that require a more compassionate approach: charity, education, health. This may be because these areas demand qualities they have and enjoy using. It may also be due to their interest in them.

PAs must excel at handling people, organising things and using information technology in a very pressured environment and all at once. PAs must be able to multi-task – to do several things at once, juggling several things in the air.

Handling people

If you are going to be a top PA, you must genuinely like people, because you will be in touch with them from the minute you arrive in the office until you leave, on the telephone, by fax, by e-mail and letter. Some will certainly try your patience (they could be the boss/es) but you'll need to be able to get on with them all and encourage them to give their best if they are helping you out.

Top PAs must be strong communicators, effective team players and good listeners. It helps to have a thick skin because you'll certainly have to deal with some people who have huge egos. We all have our off days, and bosses and those you work with are no exception. As an ambassador for your boss(es) and your company, the way you handle people is important, not least because it can help strengthen the working relationship between you. The ability to speak and write clearly and concisely is vital, because most of those you are dealing with will be extremely busy and time will be of the essence for them. With experience, you'll be able to tell when you pick up the telephone which callers have time for small talk, which means you can move your working relationship along a bit, and those who don't because they're frantically busy. You'll need the ability to chase up people who don't do what they're supposed to do when they should. This means chasing up very senior people who are part of a working group or committee just as much as the courier who still hasn't come to collect that urgent package. You'll iron out what callers really want from your boss, especially if they aren't known to you; and get rid of them with care and tact where necessary, while maintaining the reputation of the company. A strong customer-service ethic – wanting to help others – is essential.

It's important to be able to develop effective working relationships with other people, and to be able to persuade and influence them. PAs will liaise with people at every level, from drivers, couriers, airline staff, and support staff within their own organisation, to PAs in other companies, as well as very senior people – chief executives, chairmen and chairwomen, government ministers, the inevitable sales rep hoping for a word in the boss's ear. All have to be dealt with in a professional manner, the PA acting as a gatekeeper and ensuring the salespeople get routed to the right department, or strengthening the link between the chairman and the boss. It's essential to use the right tone, language, manner and words for your audience, be they at the end of an e-mail or fax, telephone or letter. You'll never know who is going to be on the phone when you pick it up, from your mother, to a chairman or major client in a strop and wanting the boss who's on a transatlantic flight and unreachable for the next eight hours. A firm hand is a must, especially if the boss is in a meeting and cannot be disturbed, despite the pressure on the other end of the line. Finally, active listening skills are essential if you are to understand what people are really telling you behind their words. It's what people don't say, as much as what they do say, that matters.

Some PA roles are more people-oriented than others. If you supervise and train staff, you will get to know them quite well. If you greet people as customers or clients, then you'll spend less time with them but your customer care skills will need to come to the fore. Above all, you must enjoy working with people and be prepared to take them in all their various guises. It's essential to have a passion for seeking to help them, and be friendly. PAs need to be cheerful and smiling, positive and helpful, while maintaining a professional front.

Organisation and planning skills

PAs organise a variety of things on a world-wide basis, including videoconferences, conference calls, meetings, travel itineraries, interviews, the boss's day and conferences – and more! This brings you into contact with a wide variety of people in and out of the company. It's essential to have an eye for detail and a passion for making sure that things go right first time. The more senior or well known your boss, the more important this is – there's no room for mistakes at the top. It reflects badly on you, too, and wastes your time and energy putting things right. Planning and organising things means thinking them through. You need to walk through every aspect of those things you plan in your mind; the more senior your boss or the greater the number of people who are affected, the more certain you need to be that you have done everything you can to see that things are going to run smoothly.

Looking after your bosses increasingly means making every minute count and planning their day – and yours – meticulously but without your bosses realising the planning that has gone into their trip behind the scenes to make sure that everything goes smoothly. PAs need to be organised, because many bosses aren't. 'If I was going to give my boss a piece of paper which was important, I always photocopied it first. Don't ask me how, but she always managed to lose the original within a few minutes of it being in her hand' (Amanda, PA to an author). Some bosses are incredibly organised themselves, but not all. PAs also need to be able to establish systems to assist in the organisation of the office and the boss – databases, files, libraries of information and so on.

Using information technology

At the very least, good PAs need a thorough understanding of how information technology can benefit an organisation and individuals. Top PAs need to develop an excellent knowledge of software packages such as Word, Excel (for spreadsheets), PowerPoint (for presentations), Access (databases) and desktop publishing (DTP). They also need to be able to use e-mail and the Internet. The latter will enable you to monitor client affairs, check the news, access online databases, have discussions, search for relevant products and materials, research a project or presentation, download software and access research and business figures. You can book travel, do your purchasing and check your boss in for a flight. You'll also need to know how to manage computer files.

Some employers fuss about typing speeds more than others; this depends on how much typing the role will involve. Overall, accuracy is more important than speed. Many PAs are given the responsibility of doing the final formatting for documents such as letters, because they know how to make them look good. The faster you can type, the faster you'll be able to get through your workload.

How much IT knowledge you have will depend on the role you want: some PAs want a very IT-focused role, creating, maintaining and improving IT systems, and overseeing IT projects. Some roles will demand expertise in particular packages. Some employers demand specialist skills, such as financial service organisations, which may demand that PAs need a good working knowledge of Reuters and Bloomberg; or media and publishing companies, which want people with DTP skills such as Adobe InDesign, Illustrator, PhotoShop and MS Publisher.

Case studies: There are different angles to IT

Sandy, PA to three headhunters

My job is to maintain the database system, which keeps track of everybody who has ever registered with us, and those we have found out about, like non-executive directors, chairmen, CEOs, chief financial officers, directors of sales and marketing, IT, HR – you name it, they're on our database and from a wide range of sectors, too. A major part of my role is to check it's up to date. As headhunters, it reflects badly on us if we send Christmas cards to people who moved on ages ago – we're supposed to know where everybody is! I established the database and am always suggesting ways to improve the system and update it, so the directors will have faster access to the information they need to find. It's become 'my' system, I suppose.

Paul, PA/project manager to the managing director of a paper company

I coordinated the office move and even found the premises. My bosses left everything to me – from building location, to setting up the IT systems, to the office furniture, because we wanted a complete overhaul of how the thing looked. Now I'm in charge of purchasing any office equipment we need and I'm also the IT person – if people have a problem, they come to me and I fix it. I've developed a real niche as a result.

So consider how computer- and systems-oriented you want your job to be. Some organisations are very systems-oriented indeed – perhaps everything you do is done on a computer, from booking flights and hotels to doing the expenses. This may suit some people but not others. If you're a computer freak, you may be the one people come to in the office with their IT problems. If you're not a computer buff, then perhaps you'd look for a role where the computer will facilitate your work but not be the be-all and end-all of the job.

What other skills do you particularly want to use on the job?

Individual PAs have their own flair for particular skills they prefer to use over others. Aside from the generic skills outlined above, each role has a different slant, often depending on the job your boss or team has or the sector you're in. You may have projects to do in your own right, such as organising a conference, or creating a Web page and maintaining it. While one PA may relish managing budgets, another may prefer to be involved in selecting and training new recruits. This chapter will help you delve further into the sort of role you want in terms of the skills you want to use. We all have our strengths. Audit yours, and you'll be better placed to seek out the right job for you.

Some roles place a heavy emphasis on doing a specific task more than others from the start, and this will usually be stressed in any job adverts at the recruitment stage – 'This position involves meeting and conference organisation.' In this example, a key feature at interview would be to find out how many conferences you would organise a year, their size and location, and what sort of people attend them, to give you an idea of exactly how large an aspect this will play in a role. You could ask, 'What percentage of my time do you envisage would be spent organising conferences?' and 'Do you see the number of conferences held increasing or decreasing? What will impact on that?' Then you'd also need to find out what internal support you could expect from the organisation, to help make your life easier, or whether you're really going to get landed with the task *tout seul* – alone. Other roles have no such specific tasks at the outset, but the PA may suggest them as she identifies a need for them to be done, having been in the role for a time.

The list that follows reflects how much the skills PAs use have expanded. Look back on your past work experience, hobbies, interests and favourite subjects at school, college and/or university. Identify those you enjoyed doing and which you're particularly good at. If you're doing this with a friend, compare notes. Ask family and friends what they think you're good at, too. You'll soon see that some of us have a better head for figures, or find it easy to use computers, while others prefer to do research. Pinpoint the skills you particularly want to use, and then you can look for a role that will use them straight away or give you the opportunity to develop them. This means thinking about what tasks you want to undertake in the short and long term at work:

- budgeting;
- administering systems;
- creating and producing, eg documents, newsletters, presentations, Web sites;
- making recommendations about systems and office management, such as suppliers;
- maintaining records, such as a membership database;
- analysing data and setting out your findings appropriately;
- preparing quality research documents;
- resourcing highly sensitive information;
- arranging highly confidential interviews;
- choosing and using equipment and technology;
- dealing with finances and financial information;
- handling difficult situations and people;
- taking and transcribing shorthand;
- booking meeting rooms and board rooms;
- checking and actioning e-mails;
- distributing information/literature/documents;
- meeting and greeting clients and customers;
- preparing weekly/monthly reports;
- providing customer services;
- collating information for business units;
- coordinating the printing of directories and newsletters;
- coordinating meeting room and conference facilities;
- dealing with the mail and couriers;
- establishing a new company and premises;
- improving internal processes;
- organising filing systems;
- servicing committees;
- translating reports and documents;
- handling enquiries from the public;
- booking appropriate restaurants;
- negotiating rates with travel agents, hotels;
- carrying out research on the Internet;

- mail-merging letters;
- ordering stationery;
- coordinating a team;
- building up a solid rapport with clients;
- proofreading;
- looking after company car policies;
- ensuring that laws and regulations are applied;
- handling correspondence;
- liaising with VIPs;
- being in charge of corporate hospitality;
- researching and producing reports/statistics/economy and company information;
- managing projects;
- recruiting, training, coaching, mentoring and supervising staff;
- taking minutes at meetings;
- making travel arrangements/complex itineraries;
- organising visas;
- diary management;
- welcoming, meeting and greeting people;
- planning lunches/meals/conferences;
- promoting the business;
- organising rotas;
- planning parties;
- running a campaign;
- any other you can think of.

Many of the skills in the list above can easily develop into self-employment opportunities on a full-time basis. You could develop a role as a specialist PA, perhaps studying for relevant qualifications in your chosen sector or a generic one:

- *Marketing assistant.* Marketing assistants help with trade shows and event planning; they create and update presentations and track budgets and expenses. They help in all aspects of business development, including the production of corporate literature and Web design. Some small companies need PAs with strong marketing and public relations abilities.
- *Sales secretary.* Sales secretaries may support a number of sales representatives who are on the road, visiting prospective clients. They process expenses, make travel arrangements and

hotel bookings, and arrange meetings with clients. They track sales progress and produce spreadsheets and graphs for presentations and reports. They are an important linchpin and focus in pulling teams together, giving the reps contact with home, and reminding them they are part of a team.

▪ *Trading floor assistant.* Trading floor secretaries are particularly busy, frequently with 30 to 40 lines to answer, arranging global travel itineraries and ordering foreign currency.

▪ *Farm secretary.* Farm secretaries have a passionate interest in the countryside and a head for figures and administration. Farmers need full and accurate financial data on their farm's performance, and farm secretaries need specialist knowledge as well as good administrative and accountancy skills. They make sure the farmer benefits from all the various grants and subsidies available and that the correct forms are filled in for the Ministry of Agriculture. There is good scope for going free-lance and setting up your own business as a farm secretary.

▪ *Legal secretary.* Legal secretaries must have an interest in law and how it works. They support fee earners, who demand different levels of support. Some simply want somebody to do the typing in a 9-to-5, no-hassle role. Others want PAs who will become very much involved in client liaison, diary arrangements and organising events.

▪ *Medical secretary.* Medical secretaries need a strong interest in health and people, but they need to keep the consultants' needs and those of the patient in mind at the same time when handling both. You can convert to being a medical secretary from a 'general' one; and some nurses also become medical secretaries. Both legal and medical secretaries must be accurate and pay great attention to detail, and be sensitive to confidentiality.

Some of these roles can lead to full-time positions focusing on one aspect of the PA job you particularly enjoy, such as:

▪ *Roadshow coordinator.* This role involves coordinating a road-show for a corporate organisation, such as an investment bank, whereby the client goes 'on the road' to meet investors and shareholders. This involves booking hotels, conference rooms, travel and cars, and producing complex schedules and itineraries.

▨ _Conference organiser_. This involves finding and booking the venue, buying in speakers, doing the marketing for it, seeing to refreshments, etc. You work closely with the venue and send out invitations, put the programme together and oversee the organisation of the conference from the outset to completion.

So identify the skills you want to use at work, and you're more likely to find a role you enjoy and are good at.

I want a job that will enable me to use my talents!

You may have particular skills and talents that you particularly want to use on the job, such as languages. Bilingual secretaries are in demand, both in the UK, where bosses need their language expertise (as many bosses have solely English), and elsewhere, where perhaps bosses have a very limited ability to speak English and want somebody who can talk to English-speaking clients. Bilingual PAs use their languages constantly to translate documents, send e-mails, take telephone calls, write faxes and attend client meetings. Any organisation that has non-English-speaking clients needs people who speak their clients' language and understand their culture. Non-traditional languages are more likely to be demanded by banking, legal, engineering and shipping companies, especially for temps, where companies have secured contracts for a short period of time. Bilingual PAs should be interested in other cultures and, particularly, you should know a bit about business culture in, say, Italy, if you speak Italian, and the way of life in the country, its prize achievements and history. You're likely to be speaking on the phone to people in their language in their country, and it helps to develop the relationship with them if you can talk about what their plans are for the weekend and so on.

Small companies such as art galleries and dealers, architects and building companies may offer the opportunity to travel on the job. Oil and gas companies are another outlet. Institutions such as the United Nations, NATO, the World Bank and the World Health Organisation, as well as the European Union, embassies, international publishing and travel firms, investment banks and the media all need bilingual and trilingual secretaries.

Different sectors and roles require their own qualities and approach

Different organisations and sectors require workers with their own skills and abilities over and above the transferable skills mentioned above. They may demand people who could fit into any of these categories shown in Figure 4.1.

If we delve deep into these categories, you will see that certain types of work have a strong relationship to them, such as:

▧ *caring* – teaching, training, health and social work, probation, careers companies, charity;
▧ *social* – leisure, hotels, clubs, party organisation and private clubs, public relations, entertainment, sporting clubs;
▧ *practical/technical* – construction, architecture, surveying, scientific, manufacturing, industrial, mining, oil and gas, forestry, engineering;
▧ *professional* – banking, law, accountancy, insurance, management consultancy;

Figure 4.1 Skills and abilities

▨ _business support_ – marketing, information technology, recruitment, human resources, e-commerce, conference and event planning;
▨ _community_ – government, politics, welfare organisations, the church, housing associations, police force, security, prisons;
▨ _creative_ – design, media, publishing, the arts, fashion, gardens, historical associations, public relations, journalism, museums;
▨ _commercial_ – businesses, e-commerce, retail, property, agricultural, logistics and transport companies, football clubs.

Few of us belong purely to one group. People who work in media are very social _and_ creative. The caring sector has taken on a more professional and businesslike approach in the way it conducts its affairs in order to survive. Community organisations such as the prison service and police forces need to have a caring, social face because of the amount of people they deal with. The professionals who work in them usually chose them because of their commitment to and belief in the values of the sector. For example, if you were to say, 'I want to give something back to the community and society', then you might want to work for a society with the values shown in Table 4.1.

Table 4.1 Values and organisations of the community sector

Values of the community sector	Associated organisations
Older people are highly valued, and have lives that are rich and voices that are heard.	Social services, charities for the elderly such as Age Concern
Every child can reach his or her potential, regardless of the start in life.	Nurseries, schools, further education and specialist colleges, central bodies relating to education and training such as the Department for Education and Skills
People should have social justice and human rights, and be free from discrimination in the sphere of law and practice.	Social work, legal firms with an interest in social policies, government, charities
Homelessness should be prevented.	Charities, local government, social welfare

'I want to do something to help others'

For the PA, much depends on how much you want to work in something that is important and valuable to you. You may have a burning desire to do something about the state of the world we live in, in which case you might work for the government, local politics, international welfare organisations and charities. PA work will give you a chance to make your contribution, to make a difference, to go home feeling as though you've done something that bettered the lives of one or more individuals.

Case study: I love this because it's worth while
Sharon, PA to three consultants

My day is really busy but I love it because I go home feeling as though I've done something really worth while. I get in in the morning and check the diaries for the consultants to see who is coming in, and look through their e-mail systems to see if there's anything I can handle. I open the post, which may include X-rays and test results for patients from other hospitals or departments in ours.

My day then varies from making appointments for people who call in, typing letters – I do medical shorthand – chasing test results, liaising with GPs and making sure that patients' details are kept up to date. We get lots of people calling in who are very anxious, and some can get quite irate if they don't get what they want. I have to balance their needs against my consultants'. I manage the claims forms so liaise a lot with insurance companies. I check that fees owing to the consultants are paid and I meet and greet patients – some are very nervous when they come in, so you need a reassuring, mature manner to do this job. I have occasionally helped by holding a patient's hand while they are being examined or having a procedure done.

Maintaining the patients' confidentiality is really important in this line of work, and it can be difficult if their relatives are calling in to demand to speak to the consultant. Attention to

---

detail is absolutely essential because mistakes lead to lost lives. You have to be very calm under pressure because we do get medical emergencies and then you have to be able to judge for yourself what to do.

Medical secretaries work in the private and public sectors in hospitals, community health, general practice, research, pharmaceuticals, complementary medicine, dental practices. They are also employed in health-related industries, such as insurance, where their medical knowledge is useful. They provide support to doctors, nurses and consultants there, and also researchers in universities with medical and/or health departments. You've got to be interested in people and health, because there are so many speciality areas to choose from. Medical people have their own speciality areas, so you may decide you want to work for people who specialise in heart problems, cancer or child illnesses, infertility or respiratory diseases.

'I want to work in the private sector, focusing on the organisations and clients'

Some PAs want a more business-focused approach. Many bosses recruit their PAs not because the PAs are passionately interested in what the organisation does or have a first-class knowledge of it (although, at the higher levels, that does help), but because they are very good at what they do and the boss knows instantly that he or she and the PA will hit it off and enjoy an excellent working partnership. The PAs' pride and commitment lie in doing an excellent job and serving the boss or the team and the wider board and the organisation with dedication, because they simply like to see a job done well. They'll know enough about the industry to know where their organisation fits into the general scheme of things. In retail, parts of the role may involve going out into the shops; for example, people working for major supermarkets may go on the shop floor to meet customers, learn about the products on offer and find out what life is like 'on the shop floor'. Often these PAs start off by knowing little about the area the organisation works in, but finds that the enthusiasm of their colleagues rubs off on them. Most bosses want PAs who've worked in a similar environment, such as a FTSE 100 company, or at a particular level, such as PA to the chairman. This experience gives PAs a thorough idea of how such companies operate and experience of handling people at a very senior level.

'I'm interested in this but not as an expert; I want to work at it from a business point of view, using the skills I have'

Some PAs choose a role because it's in an area that just interests them. For example, PAs who work as assistants in an art gallery probably love art and appreciate the love clients have for it; PAs who have an art history degree plus Italian may work for an art gallery that has strong links with clients in Italy and France. PAs exist in virtually every arena of life, so you have more choice than most in terms of whom you work for. Some of these posts can be very narrow: 'An international manufacturing company seeks a PA with a knowledge of and interest in DIY products.'

Consider how much industry knowledge you want to learn. Are you keen to read trade and professional magazines, or sit with your nose glued to the *Financial Times* on your way into the office? The more you know about the products and services your organisation is selling, the more effective you'll be and the more you'll enjoy your work. You may find clients increasingly turn to you as a source of information and that the more involved you get, the more you want to learn. Additionally, you'll contribute ideas and feedback you've received from customers.

Case study: Be passionate about what you do

Julia, PA to the head of customer services in a heritage organisation

I think one of the reasons I got this job was because I spend a lot of my spare time visiting places of historical interest. I put this on my CV and we talked about it at interview, so I could

---

show that I had an idea of how these places worked, and what sort of people make them tick, and what the public think about them. Working with something I'm naturally interested in has made a big difference to the way I feel about what I do; I'm always visiting our attractions, and those of our competitors, to see what they're doing. I think I can make a greater contribution to the organisation overall and I like to think I have an input into what it can offer the public. My boss is also always asking me what I think and is very open to my ideas, so that's made me more useful to her, too.

Some more examples are shown in Table 4.2.

Many bosses are more interested in how you work with them, and what you can do and produce for them in terms of output, than in your interest in the services and products their companies promote. But the more you believe in what your organisation

Table 4.2 Combining work and interests

Your interests	Associated work
Property, France _business, commercial_	International property company with strong commercial interests in France
Food, wine _social, commercial_	Wine wholesalers, food retailers
Art history _creative, social_	Art gallery as an office manager/business assistant
Business and finance _professional, business support_	Banks, finance companies, private equity companies, insurance
Current affairs and politics, languages _community, caring_	Political organisations (local or national), MPs, MEPs, embassies
Animal welfare _caring_	Charities

61

does, services your organisation sells, and the more committed you are to its values and the values of the team around you, the better a job you will do.

What sort of approach are you comfortable with?

Think about the sort of approach you like to take and which sectors need them:

- mature;
- proactive;
- friendly;
- fun;
- lively;
- calm;
- professional;
- confident;
- social;
- sympathetic;
- businesslike;
- laid-back;
- high-energy;
- compassionate;
- caring;
- sociable;
- practical;
- fast;
- glamorous;
- by-the-book;
- friendly, welcoming;
- country-loving;
- firm;
- discreet.

As an example, if you are very discreet and firm, you could look at working for an executive search company.

Case study: When people's careers are at risk, the stakes go up

Rachel, PA in an executive search company

Generally, a lot of our work is inputting data on the PC into our in-house database and typing up candidate letters from audiotapes. You need to be a fast, accurate typist, discreet on the telephone, and able to maintain confidentiality and understand its importance to the client and to candidates you're courting. Some of the searches we do are so confidential that everything gets faxed to the CEO at home, because nobody else knows the search is being undertaken. You also have to be careful when you call people up – you can't leave the name of the organisation you're calling from, or people will know a headhunter is after somebody. When we get a new search, we have to come up with a list of names of people who may be appropriate for the post by scouring the contacts we have in our database and the news to see who is in it; then we type up a list of candidates into a presentation. We often have to call a candidate's company to check they are still working there, which can be tricky. If you're calling a company to find out if some 30 people are still working there, their switchboard can start to catch on that something is up. A major part of the job is also dealing with CVs, which come rolling in every day from hopefuls who are on the search themselves for another post. Usually, we show these to the bosses and then have to write back a letter explaining that we can't help them at the moment, or that they are being put into the database in case a future search comes up. This can be tricky when somebody who thinks their career is absolutely fantastic calls up and can't understand why we won't even interview him. It may be superb but, if we're not working on a related assignment, he'll go into the database until something comes up.

Case study: Maturity is an asset when you're handling clients

Marina, PA to a matrimonial lawyer

I went through a divorce myself, so I think I can empathise with clients because I know what they're going through. The guys I work for handle divorce custody issues and mediation cases. I did think about working with child abuse cases, but that's a particularly sensitive area and I thought it would be too much for me. It amazed me how much scope there was to diversify in law. Our company, for example, has people who specialise in housing issues, such as tenancy, conveyancing, litigation; the environment; medical negligence; media; sports law; and employment law. When I joined, I was able to spend some time in these sections to see if they were for me, but I think the matrimonial side is the one I have the most compassion for and interest in. I think maturity is a great asset, because you have to be extremely discreet and trustworthy, and very professional. Clients have to feel comfortable talking about their affairs with you. It's a very privileged role.

Legal secretaries are in demand, because of our specialist knowledge of legal terminology and procedures. Some law firms take secretaries on from professional backgrounds, which is what happened to me – I'd worked for management consultants before. I did a training course and made good friends with a couple of other new starters – one had just finished a legal secretarial course. I found it was a challenge to grasp legal technology and the ways in which legal documents have to be produced, but I've always been interested in law, so that helped. We spend a few months being float secretaries and working in different departments to get a taster for them and meet the partners there, before deciding on what suited us best. A PA's role will depend on how senior the lawyer is and the structure of the organisation. My bosses are quite senior, and want me to take some of the routine administration off their hands, so they can focus more on the law and clients. Every minute of our day counts, because it's all billed to clients.

What qualities do you have?

Allied closely to the sort of approach you prefer come the qualities you want to use on the job. Most companies want people who are going to be highly skilled, intelligent, presentable, well spoken, reliable, flexible and competent – everything really. However, most will focus on one or two qualities that are particularly important to them and you can take a hint from that as to the sort of person they're looking for.

Since so many work projects are done in teams now, employers are keen to create teams of top-flight people who will work closely together effectively. Different sectors will demand their own qualities more than others; so consider what your make-up is and what makes *you* the person you are:

- accurate under pressure;
- courteous;
- professional;
- confidential;
- practical;
- common sense;
- friendly;
- resourceful;
- mature;
- calm under pressure;
- strong character;
- can-do approach;
- diplomatic;
- good team player;
- quick-thinking;
- tenacious;
- ease of manner;
- charisma;
- leader;
- able to put people at ease;
- numerate;
- persuasive;
- imaginative;
- able to gain people's confidence;

- creative flair;
- articulate;
- ambitious;
- attention to detail;
- computer-literate;
- socially confident;
- polished;
- initiative;
- high energy level;
- sense of humour;
- discreet;
- tactful;
- flexible;
- adaptable;
- able and willing to learn;
- polite;
- committed;
- solid;
- worldly-wise;
- young;
- trustworthy;
- understanding manner;
- patient;
- practical.

Case study: Confidentiality is my middle name
Janet, works in human resources

I spend a lot of time on the telephone to headhunters and recruitment agencies who want to enter into exclusive working relationships with our companies. Since my boss is the head of HR in Europe, that involves a lot of effort on his part – and research on mine – in keeping updated with everything that is going on concerning European directives and how they might affect us. We are also responsible for the whole performance review process. It's my job to supervise the assistants and ensure they know how to handle the documentation correctly when it's given out to line managers for the review process, because it's extremely confidential. This job is always super-manic, but there are times of the year, such as the time when compensation packages are given out, when it is a nightmare. Last year, we also had the impact of September 11th to deal with, and three rounds of redundancies. My boss and I were kept extremely busy. You really have to take the good with the rough in HR, which can probably move into people's personal lives more than any other area. I take minutes of meetings and conference calls amongst the senior managers, so get to find out what's going on before anybody else in the company, which is mind-boggling if it involves stuff like redundancies and salary reviews.

Think broadly when considering the organisations that need the skills and qualities you have and the approach you prefer. This is important, because there are all sorts of hidden areas that people don't automatically think of. If you think of working in education, for example, traditionally most people would think of being a PA to a headteacher in a primary or secondary school. Broaden that thought to include colleges, universities, private training companies and local authority education departments, and you'll increase your range of opportunities and the people you'll deal with.

Look, too, at the changes being undertaken in different sectors, because they can tell you a lot about how your working day could be affected. Secretaries in education will have contact with parents, who are becoming more abusive and demanding. Tact and diplomacy, and the ability to stay calm, are crucial attributes. It's crucial to respect confidentiality and to like children. There's more to juggle because of the various government, local and school initiatives, and changes in the National Curriculum. There are more committees for heads and deputy heads to sit on, not just in school but across counties, so you're likely to be heavily involved in organising meetings.

Summary

▨ What do you want to achieve and contribute in the workplace?
▨ Think about the qualities you particularly want to use on the job.
▨ Think about the sort of people you want to be working with and for. How closely do their interests and values match yours? Could you see yourself looking forward to work in such an environment?

5 How and where do you want to be employed?

How relationships between you and the company have changed

A few years ago, there was little doubt about the type of relationship you would have with an employer. A permanent job with lifelong security – and little chance of career breaks, changing career or taking a sabbatical. Although many negative things are said about there being 'no job for life any more', it's important to look at the plus sides. How many of us now would really want a permanent job lasting our entire working lives? If we were offered a job 'for life', most of us would opt for the riskier approach that at least gives us greater freedom. And in fact, in a day when job security is no more, what counts is your ability to stay in control of your life overall:

▓ *financial control* – knowing what your situation is and how much of a security blanket you have for now (in case you're made redundant) and in the future (what will you do for money when you retire or can no longer work?);
▓ *control of your career* – driving it to where you want to be so that it gives you the sort of lifestyle you want and need;
▓ *control of your life* – knowing how you want to fill your time so that you get more out of it, and having the right amount of time to relax, travel, be with friends, do a course or voluntary work or whatever you want.

At the heart of the matter lies the control issue: knowing how to take control and secure the sort of relationship we want with an employer, from the length of time we stay with them, to the hours we work, to the location. Much depends on your own personal circumstances, but also on how well informed you are on things that affect your life. For example, how much do you know about new legislation, which could increase the opportunities open to you or threaten your lifestyle? Or new financial products that will make your money work harder for you? Having information to hand, or knowing how to get it, plays a key role in ensuring you feel in control of your life and boosting your confidence.

Understanding what the choices are in these three areas of control – finance, career and life – and knowing which we prefer and why gives us the ability to lead a very full life. They are all strongly linked. Control over our finances – not spending more than we are earning – means we are less likely to fall into debt. The career we choose – say working in investment banking – may bring us lots of money (financial control) but at the same time take away some of the control we have over our lifestyle. (Investment banking traditionally involves lengthy hours.) The knowledge we have about all these issues enables us to build a concrete life with more of the things we want in it. This chapter seeks to focus on the ways we can be employed, and the locations we might work in.

The number of ways we can be employed has increased, giving us far more choice and the opportunity to fit the career in with life ambitions. Most people have a 'permanent' post, with the traditional 9 to 5, Monday to Friday and four or five weeks' holiday a year. Some people make a career out of temporary work, partly because they like the flexibility but also because it can fit in with their own goals. Others go freelance, running their own business, or become portfolio workers, where they neatly juggle two part-time jobs working for different employers, or have a part-time job to keep the cash coming in while they're building up their own business.

The first part of this chapter will focus on two particular ways you can build a career as a top PA outside of permanent employment: as a career temp or as a freelance PA. The second part will focus on where you might work, and consider how much of an international flavour you want to seek out. If you know what you want, it's much easier to plot your path to make sure you get it.

Be a career temp

Currently, UK companies hire a million agency temps every week, enough to warrant their own National Temporary Workers Week, generally held in October. (Visit www.tempweek.uk.com for more details.) Temporary workers are employed in a wide range of careers, covering while people are off sick or on holiday, but also because they have a particular skill the company requires or because the company needs more hands on deck as they've just won a new contract. Employing temps allows companies to add and delete staff as they need them. Scary as that may sound, and the fear is that Monday will loom on the distance and you'll have no work, top PAs who temp usually find the problem is trying to have a break between assignments. Their abilities to handle people and to hit the ground running, combined with their technical know-how and flexible approach, are in demand. Enter the career temp, who makes a long-term career out of temping and is a highly skilled individual.

As assignments can last anywhere from a morning to several months, temping can be particularly useful if:

- you have particular ties, such as children, at certain times of the year;
- your partner gets transferred a lot while working;
- you like the challenge of adapting to the unknown and proving yourself in record time;
- you can relate to all sorts of people and new situations quickly, and learn fast;
- you like to decide when you work and relish that flexibility;
- you fit it in to complement one career or while working towards a new one;
- you arrange to temp so that you can fit things into your life that you want to do.

The downsides of temping or doing contract work is that you don't get the perks permanent staff get. Legislation surrounding the employment of temporary workers is changing all the time. It's in your interests to watch for new EU employment regulations, which might affect the way organisations employ temps. Although initially it may sound as if they will make life easier, in the long run they could mean the cost of employing temps and contract workers becomes too great. This could force employers to create new ways of taking on and shedding staff at very short notice and filling skill gaps, and could threaten the career temp's opportunities to work. For information on your rights as a temporary or contract worker, visit www.troubleatwork.org.uk/ShowTopics.asp.

Case study: Be very good at what you do – think of yourself as a company
Carla, a career temp

If you're going to temp, my advice is to never know what to expect – you've got to be flexible and adaptable. Because things change so fast for organisations, what the agency told you on Friday afternoon about what you'd be doing on Monday is often no longer relevant by the time you turn up. I've arrived at assignments expecting to work for one team and been asked to move to another by the company because I've just got more experience, or more relevant skills, or the guy is particularly difficult to handle and they know I'm good with that sort of person. I've worked for guys with really bad tempers, who no one would stay with for long. Then I had to make sure I didn't get landed with him for months on end. You have to keep control.

It's important not to be a prima donna in this line of work. You have to go with the flow and be professional about it, but you have to look after yourself, too. I've done all sorts of tasks when temping, from high-level stuff to the low. I spent a week organising a guy's filing system. Because I was there, and visible, the company offered me another assignment working for a senior guy the following week for two months. One of the essential skills you have to have is self-knowledge so that you can say very quickly what your unique selling points are. I constantly try to pinpoint mine by asking those I've worked for what I've done particularly well; where I need to develop my skills, so that I can fill any gaps in my knowledge and skills set; and whether I've exceeded their expectations. I also think privately about what I particularly liked about the company, which helps me decide which companies I want to go back to.

If you're going to be a career temp, you need good budgeting skills so that you can build up a reserve for any times you're not working – I try to bank the equivalent of a day's pay every week. My next goal is to start looking at a personal pension plan. Once a year, I ask my agency for an increased rate – if you don't ask, you may not get. You have to look after yourself. Think of yourself as a company – Me Plc – and it becomes much easier.

Top temps add value every inch of the way. You have to prove yourself from the minute you arrive at your new assignment, which is why being a career temp is very challenging. I've built up an excellent network of contacts, developed really good people skills and can cope with anything that's thrown at me. I've handled quite a few projects, such as setting up new systems for temporary workers and setting up conferences. My IT skills have expanded tremendously – I've learnt how to do spreadsheets and use Access because I learnt on the job. As a temp, you're used to handling change because you're moving roles all the time, so it comes much easier to you. You learn how to form solid working relationships fast. Like a team of experts pulled together to work on a project, who have to focus on the task in hand, so a career temp must do the same. We are helped by the fact we can be oblivious to office politics, and can perhaps help pull teams together as an outsider.

I've had a lot of fun, met some fabulous people – and was asked back to look after the really bad-tempered guy next Monday. Luckily, I'm off to Chile for a month.

Some people eventually tire of the novelty of temping; it's exhausting being nice to people all the time, particularly if they are irritating and demanding. And yet, when it comes to signing that contract for the permanent post, it's human nature if you've been a temp for some time to have a sudden moment of thinking, 'Stop.

Am I doing the right thing? What if...?' The great thing about getting into a permanent job through temping is that you get an opportunity to put the boss or team you'd be working for – and the company – to the test first.

Go it alone!

Allied slightly to temping, because you have to prove yourself constantly and to build up a strong network of clients who want to use your services time after time, is the opportunity to go it alone. Freelance PAs work from home or telecottage centres, for individuals and small businesses, charities and local institutions, locally and globally, thanks to the Internet. (Enter the virtual assistant.) Careful research will help you determine your niche in terms of the clients you work for and the services you offer. This is not for the inexperienced, and you should be sure of your reasons for going it alone. Is it to get out of the rat race and that hideous commute, or because you've seen your boss run a business and thought, 'I could do that!'

Some of the services freelance and virtual PAs offer include:

- business letters;
- diary organisation;
- Internet research;
- Web design;
- event planning;
- Web site maintenance;
- mail merge;
- minute taking;
- newsletter publishing;
- writing;
- coaching;
- live phone answering;
- public relations;
- interpreting;
- social events/conference planning;
- training;

- travel organisation;
- database management;
- payroll administration;
- presentations;
- accountancy;
- membership database;
- screening phone calls and e-mails;
- agenda preparation;
- dog walking;
- audio-visual production;
- research;
- proofreading;
- spreadsheets;
- desktop publishing;
- coordinating meetings and travel;
- telephone answering service.

To go freelance, you must be able to form and develop client relationships through trust and delivery of high standards of service; you must be a self-starter and first-class problem solver, confident in your own ability without reassurance from others. You need a well-thought-out business plan, and the energy, determination and stamina to follow it through. Make sure you can deliver what you promise, well within the timescales you give. It's better to take on a little and deliver, and gain a reputation for being reliable, than to be known as someone who is always late. You'll need to track changes in the market, keep track of customer demands and keep up to date with those demands by being able to offer the skills set you need. Finally, you must be adaptable, flexible and reliable, and cope well with change and interruption to your home routine. You may have to sacrifice holidays and weekends in the early days as your business takes off.

To kick off, you'll need a computer with Internet access, a fax, a phone with voice-mail or answering service, and any other tools to help you deliver the sorts of services you'll be offering. If you set up your own Web site, make it simple and easy to get around – nothing will make users leave it faster than not being able to get the information they need quickly. Include contact details such as an e-mail address and business phone number and keep it up to date. One option is to set up in a telecottage centre, which enables small-business owners to share facilities such as computers, fax machines and photocopiers.

However much you plan and do your homework, eventually you have to take the risk of going from a 'secure' pay cheque and being employed, to going it alone, with the inevitable financial risks that follow, but also the immense satisfaction of running your own business and doing it your way. One of the scariest factors is taking the leap and actually starting it up. Will you cope financially? What will happen to you once you don't have the back-up of a regular salary coming in to pay the bills? Starting up your own business is a bit like skiing down a daunting slope. You've checked everything: the weather, ski conditions, lie of the slope and level of difficulty; you've talked to people who've done it. But there's still that element of risk. What will happen once you push off the edge and start off? Ultimately, if you aren't prepared to take the risk and throw yourself off that ledge, then you're always going to stay put. Do your homework. Make the decision. Throw yourself into making sure the decision was the right one.

Try to talk to people who have set up their own business to find out about the pitfalls. If they have experienced problems, see if they have any advice for you. There may be support networks in your area; details should be available from your local Learning and Skills Council (tel: 0870 900 6800; Web site: www.lsc.gov.uk; or check your local *Yellow Pages*). Local colleges run short courses in running your own business, where you'll pick up lots of useful advice. And most banks and building societies produce leaflets with advice, which you can pick up at your local branch.

For more advice and support, contact:

- www.businesslink.org for practical advice on setting up, financing and running small businesses;
- Employer's Helpline (tel: 0345 143143) – can help with basic tax matters or national insurance enquiries; also provides basic information on registering for VAT, statutory sick pay and maternity benefit;
- Federation of Small Businesses, Sir Frank Whittle Way, Blackpool Business Park, Blackpool, Lancs FY4 2FE (tel: 01253 336000; Web site: www.fsb.org.uk);

▓ Health and Safety Executive Information Line (tel: 08701 545500) – gives information and provides publications on a wide range of business, and health and safety issues; visit also www.hse.gov.uk/startup;
▓ Inland Revenue – general enquiries regarding tax matters, PAYE, expenses and benefits; call your local tax office for information; check your local phone book under 'Inland Revenue';
▓ Telecottage Association, WREN Telecottage, Stoneleigh Park, Warwickshire CV8 2RR (tel: 024 7669 6986; Web site: www.tca.org.uk);
▓ The International Association of Virtual Assistants (IAVA); visit their Web site www.iava.org.uk to get some advice from virtual assistants who've done it!

Location, location, location

When it comes down to the location you work in, most of us are less mobile than we would like. However, if you really are serious about your career, you should be prepared to move about. If you work locally, but have access to a city, you need to weigh up the cost and stresses, time and energy spent commuting into the cities for the larger salaries against the lower wages and less stressful journeys you may have if you have a short distance to work. The opportunities available to you will depend on the organisations available in your area, the salary you're seeking, how much travelling you're prepared to do before you start work and after you finish, and how much of your pay cheque you're ready to commit to commuting. If you want to work for a FTSE 100 company, you may be committed to working in a city.

Pay makes a difference, and varies according to the sector, the region you're working in, the level of people you're working for and your skills and experience. Current market trends will also affect any salaries offered to new staff. The location makes a difference too, and, in London, rates vary between the West End and the City (see Table 5.1).

If you're thinking of moving regions within the UK, check out:

Table 5.1 Varying rates of pay

	Annual salary	Temp rate	Hours
City	£26–32,000	£11–14/hour	8.30–6.30
West End	£22–25,000	£9–11/hour	9.00–5.30
West Sussex	£10–15,000	£5.50–8/hour	9.00–5.30

▓ recruitment companies, which frequently undertake salary reviews, such as www.joslinrowe.com;

▓ www.upmystreet.com where you can check out property prices, crime rates and local authority services;

▓ www.britishjobs.net, which lets you search for job opportunities by town and county, giving details of each town's major employers, schools, facilities in the area and local transport;

▓ local newspapers and job centres, which should have vacancies on the Internet and should give you an idea of the salaries to expect.

Going abroad

Another exciting option is to work abroad and give your career an international flavour. You also acquire this to some extent by working with colleagues from all over the world, so, even if you never leave Slough, you do at least get an exposure to people from other countries. Working with people from different nationalities requires particular skills, such as a cultural awareness, a knowledge of what it's like to work across boundaries and the problems you might encounter.

There are a number of points to think about when working overseas:

▓ Are you the right sort of person to work abroad, or should you limit yourself to your two weeks a year in the Costa del Sol where you'll have access to fish and chips and hotels that cater for the British tourist? Ask yourself questions such as:
  – How quickly do you seek to go out of your way to meet people from other countries?

- How do you cope when things aren't going to plan?
- Are you naturally interested in how other countries operate?
- Do you tend to give up easily?
- Can you cope when the going gets tough?
- Do you have a good support system?
- Are you a risk taker?
- Can you handle things when they are done differently to the way you would do them?

If you can answer 'yes' to most of these, then start packing!

▓ Where do you want to work abroad? If you want to go purely for fun, then the world is your oyster. Think about the type of work you want. Do you want a break from PA work, or to use being abroad as a chance to add something different to build your career and boost your CV? If you work in a city, there are more likely to be international companies there who need bilingual secretaries. You may decide to move somewhere where you have friends and/or family already.

▓ How far are you prepared to adapt to a new lifestyle? For example, could you work in a country where alcohol is forbidden or where there are strict laws outlining what work women can and can't do?

▓ What do you want to achieve? Some countries will enable you to save a lot of money while you're away, such as Saudi Arabia, where you might benefit from a tax-free salary, free accommodation, free flights home every year, plenty of annual leave, free medical care and social facilities.

▓ How long do you want to work abroad for? Is this all about doing some travelling, working your way around doing anything you can to avoid dipping too much into your savings, or do you want to stay in one spot and become immersed in the local culture? Six months is usually too short, almost like an extended holiday. A year gives you a better length of time to become acquainted with the locals and their habits and really get settled in. If you're learning a language and want to perfect your linguistic skills, a year at least will be essential.

▓ Do you want to improve your language skills while you're away? We all have different linguistic skills, ranging from none at all, through being able to order a glass of wine in the 'second' language, enough to get by and then a working knowledge of another language, to native, which means that it should be your first language. If English is your only language, all is not lost. You still have plenty of options.

- Do you want to travel as part of the job you have in the UK? While this option always sounds good, it is also overrated. Be prepared for long working days, leaving you little time to sightsee. The focus when travelling abroad as part of the job is to achieve what you need to in the shortest space of time possible, so that you can get back to the office. Shopping may be limited to grabbing the accessories you need at the airport and raiding the duty-free shop on your way back.

In a small world, where the Internet has made it so much easier to make contact with the tiniest company on the other side of the earth, so have regulations and bureaucracy come time and time again in the way of aspirations and dreams. Don't let that put you off. If you're prepared to be flexible – and, let's face it, you have to be when you're working abroad – you will find a job overseas.

Finding a job in another country

Working abroad certainly will give your CV and your life some colour. In response to EU developments, career services and local, national and European governments have sought to make access to information easier with printed materials (check your public library) and Web sites such as:

- Careers Europe – www.careerseurope.co.uk;
- Eurodesk Information Service – www.eurodesk.org;
- www.talent4europe.com – 16 leading European newspapers and careers sites have created this site, which connects to over 40,000 jobs.

Some recruitment agencies have partnerships with sister agencies in other countries. Some have a particular focus, such as the Middle East, Europe, Australia, New Zealand or South Africa. You can find agencies with an international reach in newspapers and on the Internet. You could also consider working for international organisations such as the United Nations, NATO or the World Health Organisation. If you are in a job where you have lots of people around you from all over the world, they may have contacts who can help you – especially if they can tell their friends and business contacts that you're a good person to have on board. Get in touch with local professional organisations for secretaries before you go – they will be able to give you any handy hints on local recruitment practices.

It's important to do some research on this point, because CVs have different emphases in different countries – in some places, you mustn't talk about your hobbies, and in others you must. The How To series *Living and Working in...*, available in bookshops, careers services and public libraries, has useful pointers. In some countries, the chamber of commerce is a powerful tool in your hunt to make contacts and land that job.

If you're hoping to join a global organisation in the likelihood that you'll be posted abroad, you might be tempted to ask for a transfer elsewhere. Unfortunately, many countries have a policy of employing nationals first, taking on outsiders only when their own can't fill the job. One possibility is to see if you can take a sabbatical for six months or so. Test the climate and choose the right time to bring the subject up. List the positive points of your goal to go abroad and how the company will benefit from your refreshed point of view and enhanced communication skills.

Before you go:

▨ Find out as much as you can about the business, political and social culture of your intended country before you go, such as working hours, unsaid rules regarding dress, formality, lunch hours and so on. Read up on its history and geography and try to study local customs. If you can say even 'hallo', 'goodbye' and 'thank you' in the local language, your efforts will be appreciated.

▨ Check visa requirements with the embassy to see if there are any you need to meet, such as proof of funding, a work permit or return airline ticket home. If you are working for a company overseas that has recruited you, they may take care of this sort of thing. Otherwise, you're on your own. Don't fall foul of visa regulations.

▨ Check health requirements with your GP to see whether there are any jabs you should have; and get some health insurance.

81

Check the small print – will the insurance cover you for your flight home, for example? If you're going to take part in dangerous sports, will you need to extend your insurance?

▓ Read the small print in your contract of employment and get legal advice if you're not sure what it says. It is easy to overlook contracts of employment in the excitement of working abroad. Make sure you thoroughly understand what you're signing; ask for extra time to sign it if you need to consult someone. Read between the lines to make sure you understand the terms of the contract as your new employer understands it. Much gets lost in translation.

▓ Find out about working conditions in the country you are going to – do you know a bit about the business culture and what limitations if any will be imposed on you because of your sex, religion or anything else?

▓ Look at your home base. What will happen to your home while you are away? Find someone who will forward mail to you. Work out how you will cover payments such as mortgages and standing orders. Give your address (e-mail and snail mail) to those who need it. And check what will happen to your old job when you get back.

And finally...

Before you go, you may have twinges of nerves. The most wonderful person you've ever met in your life might suddenly appear the week before you're due to go and you suddenly think, 'Oh, God, am I doing the right thing?' If the person is that brilliant, he or she will wait for you to come back, write, phone, e-mail and even visit you.

Case study: Give yourself time to settle in

Tina, executive PA to the managing director of a shipping company, Marbella

When you arrive, give yourself time to settle in. For the first few weeks, you may feel as though you're having a

---

marvellous time, as if you are on holiday. Then you'll begin to realise that you're not just there for a few weeks, but longer than that. Differences between your new country and yours will intensify; you may find things more frustrating and irritating for a while, and long for things and people familiar. I found I wanted to be with people from the UK, and it was hard to stay away from them. Once you're in a group of them, it becomes increasingly difficult to meet the natives, as it's much easier to stick to what you know. Stick your neck out, and make efforts to get to know the locals. Treat people well, use some of the local lingo, get to know local habits, and the harder times will pass. Strangely, it's the hardest times when you sit in a bar thinking, 'What am I doing this for?' that tend to be the most rewarding, those when you grow in strength as a person and really come to realise how resilient you are – but generally only after you've come out of them and look back on them some time later.

While you're there, do:

- keep in touch with people back at home, including your old office (you may want to approach them for a job when you get back);
- be sensitive to cultural differences;
- expect the hours and working conditions to be different;
- give yourself time to settle in.

Don't:

- say things are better or worse than in your own country – say they're different;
- spend too much time with people from your own country – the whole point of going is to meet new people;
- expect temping agencies and situations to work the same way they do at home.

When it all ends and you suddenly know it's time to come home to your roots, the feeling may grow gradually or it may hit you suddenly with great power one morning. That's the time to listen to your gut instinct.

It's not just the big global companies that have international opportunities. Find a company seeking to expand its business and you'll increase your chances of getting a foothold post away. Some of the best opportunities to get immersed in from an international point of view are with small companies that really have to make the best of everybody's resources. It's that hands-on approach again.

Travelling on the job

Top PAs – particularly those with strong language skills who can make up for the boss's lack thereof – are now viewing travel as part of the job and are considering it part of their working lives to undertake activities such as:

- arranging a meeting in a European city, going with their boss to ensure that everything goes smoothly and providing PA back-up while the meeting takes place;
- going with a group of PAs to provide secretarial back-up while their bosses are at an international conference;
- acting as couriers and taking vital documents to their boss to ensure that they arrive on time;
- sitting in on a client meeting abroad that they have set up, and taking minutes and notes on a laptop;
- setting up a new office in another country for their company because they have the language skills and they know the systems and can recruit and train new staff;
- moving with their boss if he or she gets transferred.

Some organisations employ staff of all different nationalities in one office. Show on your CV that you relate well to people from other countries and that you appreciate the problems and misunderstandings that can arise from communication across cultures. It will enhance your ability to pull people together in teams, as you take into account time differences, corporate hospitality expectations, the way conflicts are dealt with, in dealing with people and doing your job.

If you're surrounded by international people, use every chance you've got to learn new sentences of business phrases. The British are often particularly lazy at this sort of thing, but our European peers are generally delighted if we try out our languages on them and will be happy to help us improve our linguistic abilities. Learn a new sentence every day and you'll soon build up an impressive repertoire of business language.

Summary

▨ Think about where and how you want to work – be sure of how far you want to travel to get to work.

▨ Be open to ways to give your job plenty of colour and get as much experience as you can.

▨ Try to decide whether an international placement will feature in your careers plan. Plot to achieve whatever it is you decide on.

6 *Key skills and attributes*

Chapter 4 touched on the basic skills you need to be a good PA – handling people, using information technology and organising and planning things. You'll need excellent transferable skills:

- time management;
- assertiveness;
- business awareness;
- planning your own day;
- prioritising the workload;
- working with a minimum of supervision;
- leadership skills.

These have become more important as secretaries have spent less time typing and more time organising bosses and teams. Key essential qualities include: confidentiality, loyalty, honesty, reliability, flexibility and being a strong team player. Chapter 4 talked about handling people, using information technology and organising things. This chapter looks at other key skills PAs must have.

The ability to multi-task

The ability to handle several things at once is essential at this level. PAs certainly need to be able to juggle a lot of things very quickly in a fast-moving environment while keeping extremely calm and remaining professional. Several years' experience will fine-tune these abilities to the point where you can use them smoothly and almost without thinking. Instead of struggling to think about things and looking in panic at your 'to do' list (most of which will have come from the boss), you'll eventually have a 'to do' list that you've mostly drawn up yourself. You willingly take on responsibility without being asked.

Any skills you can acquire that will enable you to work at great speed will help. The debate on the usefulness of shorthand continues, and it's true that many employers don't request it any more, but, in the case study below, Sharon echoes the views of many PAs.

Case study: Shorthand can help move things faster

Sharon, PA in public relations

When I was at secretarial college, I learnt Pitman 2000 shorthand and most of my early jobs involved a lot of shorthand transcription, taking letters and memos and then typing them up. Now, I don't take dictation as much as I used to, but I still use my shorthand as much as ever, to remind myself of things I need to do, to take notes as my boss leaves me a list of things to do: especially useful if time is short – to take telephone messages, that sort of thing. If I hadn't learnt it, I suppose I wouldn't have missed it – but I'm really glad I've got it. The pace of the working day means I can fit more in, because I save time making notes. It's also useful for confidential things, because nobody else can read my shorthand.

Working intelligently and meticulously

In working through your day, it's important to work intelligently and meticulously, paying great attention to detail. If you assume things are going to go well without putting any effort in, then they are more liable to go wrong. Think things through and you'll have less stress. Remember, top PAs are paid to _think_.

Case study: Plan diligently

Michael, PA/project manager in IT

I'm meticulous about planning my bosses' day and really ensuring that everything goes right. If they're travelling, for example, it's not enough to book the flight and the car to get them to the airport. When they're off travelling, I take into account factors like:

▓ what traffic problems they are likely to encounter for the time of the day they are going to the airport – I get advice from the taxi or car company;

▓ the time of day they are going to the airport – will it be in rush hour?

▓ whether they are flying economy or business or first class – it makes a difference to check-in times;

▓ how much time will they need for check-in – can I check them in by telephone or online?

▓ are there any special events taking place which could affect traffic, such as strikes, marches or anniversaries?

▓ on the day, the weather – if it's pouring with rain, the traffic will be heavier than usual, so they'll need longer to get there;

▓ transfer times between terminals if they have a connecting flight – some huge airports need more time than you think to do this; if time is tight, I check out the next available flight and make sure that the tickets are transferable from one airline to another.

I always check the progress of the flight to get a landing time – it means I can change any arrangements we've made when they land to fit in if the flight is late. It also means I'm ready with telephone messages and urgent e-mails requiring attention when they call in after landing.

You have to be able to think fast in this job. It's also useful to know what the service providers can do for you: find out what facilities airlines offer business travellers, such as showers at airports, early check-in facilities, fax machines in airport lounges – it can save a huge amount of time and enable you to build more into a day.

Another important skill to have is that of project management. As the workplace becomes increasingly results-oriented, the ability to manage projects will yield results and boost your confidence. You'll be able to talk about what you've achieved in a language others understand. The best way to approach projects is to break them down into small, manageable tasks, so that rather than have one huge whole you have 10 small parts to do. Ask for help along the way from those whose knowledge in a particular area is better than yours, because they are dealing with similar issues every day. For example, if your project is to organise a conference, once you've found the venue, take advice from the hotel staff about it and ask them for ideas. They're used to holding conferences and will be able to give you lots of useful advice and tips.

Essential components of projects include:

- the willingness to take the thing on in the first place and the motivation to see it through to completion;
- understanding what needs to be achieved;
- sticking to the budget;
- working to a given timescale;
- knowing who else is involved and forming fast working relationships with them;
- deciding how you will know if it has been successful;
- for you personally, working out what you have learnt from the experience; and
- work out how you can build on the project you've just completed, or where you can take on another.

Attitude is everything

If you want to help others and enjoy doing so, then PA work will be right for you. 'But won't that make me a doormat?' you may be asking. Sharon says:

No, it won't, if you portray yourself as a professional. If you look like a down-trodden, lowly secretary, who doesn't care about anything around her, then you probably will feel a doormat. But people who are assertive, and interested, and committed to what they're doing, won't. There's a key difference here. If you can stay on the right side of helping others and behaving in a professional way, then you will be a cherished part of a team. PAs must be outward-looking to see how they can assist in the overall vision their organisations are seeking to achieve, and where they can add value. Think of it as achievements in business terms. Look ahead, plot your career path and go for it. Doormats don't have goals, nor are they assertive – they don't know how to say no effectively, so everything gets dumped on them.

Top PAs are far from doormats. They strive for perfection and have the energy and ambition to achieve. Top PAs get the routine stuff done before anybody notices it needs to be done – or they delegate it – because they want to get on with the brainpower stuff. They know where they're going and are focused on getting there. My boss always asks me for ideas and my opinions, which makes life all the more interesting. I can make a real contribution.

What basic experience will you need?

There are no career paths to follow in many careers any more, and that of PA is no exception. At the outset, you should know how the world of commerce and organisations work and an office functions, how to behave and how to treat colleagues and clients. An awareness of health and safety in the workplace is important. At the lower entry levels, enthusiasm, willingness to muck in and get involved, team working and the willingness and ability to learn are key to success. At higher entry levels, you'll need this knowledge, but you'll also need to display initiative, an ability to cope with change, intelligence, political and business acumen and an ability to pick things up and hit the ground running.

You should know how to write business letters and memos, faxes, reports and e-mails in such a way that they enhance your professional image while getting the job done. Key to this will be comprehending the role of sections such as human resources, sales and marketing, information technology, export and legal. You should understand how companies are organised and have an understanding of the issues companies face today and the pressures they are under.

Past work experience acquired at school and in holiday work will give you an idea of these things. Vocational courses should incorporate a period of relevant work experience too, to give you the chance to put into practice everything you've learnt. If you can undertake your work experience in the sector you're hoping to work in, you'll acquire an idea of the culture of that sector and you'll make contacts who may be able to help you and might even offer you a job. Talk to people on your course who were in different organisations afterwards and find out how their experience differed from yours. How would you react had you been placed in their position, do you think, as opposed to the one you were in? Learn from them and ponder how you would have enjoyed their experience.

Most PAs do some temping at some point, perhaps in the holidays, or as part of a college or university course, which gives them a good idea of what they're letting themselves in for and acts as a springboard into the PA arena. Most posts at senior level will demand two to five years' experience in a similar sector or environment.

Starting straight out of school, college or university

At the lower levels, such as office junior, no formal qualifications are required, although employers tend to look for good GCSEs in maths and English. From there, it's possible to go up the career ladder, especially if your employer is prepared to train you and you're willing to put the effort in. Use your local careers service company to get advice on writing a CV and interview technique, and find out which employers are particularly good at training office juniors in your area. If you went to a (secretarial) college or university, the careers service there may have strong links with one or more recruitment agencies, which will help you.

From university to the workplace

Many graduates become PAs – some 40 per cent of secretaries hold a degree. Secretarial colleges run short courses designed for graduates seeking a fast-track entry into a PA role. Your university or college careers service will have details. University helps students develop the confidence to cope with the unexpected, to cope with business people, to solve problems, to find things out for themselves and to be team players. Graduates with IT skills, good typing speeds, organisational skills and people skills, who are bright and energetic, can get into the workplace without doing fully fledged secretarial courses and often view this route as a way to get into other things, such as marketing and media, but it is important to be honest about this while looking for work. Some employers want to recruit a PA and that's that – they have no desire to recruit a PA wannabe financial whizz kid. Then again, some employers actively recruit graduates via this route, approaching agencies for people who are willing to start in a PA role and then move on and up if they can prove themselves.

Graduates get into PA work for a number of reasons: to pay off student debts, to earn some money to travel for a year 'before settling down to a career', to get a career established, to work out where their niche is in the workplace and as a 'way in' to a chosen career. Many graduates who enter the PA world discover they like it, that it meets their requirements – and so they stay.

Making use of government training schemes

If you find it difficult to get started, ask your local careers service about government training schemes such as New Deal or the Modern Apprenticeship. They may provide the opportunity you need to show an employer what you can do. There are programmes for people of all ages so, if you're returning to the job market after a break, your local job centre or Learning and Skills Council may be able to help you too. The Web site www.employ-mentservice.gov.uk will help you locate the nearest job centre to you. Most training schemes will enable you to work for vocational qualifications while gaining experience at work.

What qualifications do you need to be a PA?

Courses provide a very useful springboard to acquiring a position within the secretarial arena. They vary in length from one to two years (generally for 16- to 18-year-olds), to short, sharp 12-week courses for graduates, the mature student and returners to the workplace, or people on gap years. Most are designed to give you the technical skills you'll need, along with a good understanding of how business and commerce work. These courses will take people into different levels of work, including office junior (the school leaver), secretary and PA (A level and graduate).

The main awarding bodies offering secretarial qualifications are Pitman, OCR and the London Chamber of Commerce and Industry Examinations Board (LCCIEB), and examples of their courses have different entry levels, so that you can choose one to match your own particular needs. Most cover business administration, administration practice and text processing, so that you gain skills directly relevant to the modern office. Depending on the level of the course, you also have the opportunity to pick options that relate directly to your career interests, such as legal studies, organising conferences, recruiting and inducting staff, European studies or financial studies.

Courses should develop your initiative, enabling you to deal with a range of work-simulated situations. They should also include something on personal presentation skills, job hunting, CV writing and interview technique. Tutors should have had *recent* experience of the workplace themselves and maintained strong links with industry. Most (secretarial) colleges have links with recruitment agencies, which may be able to help you find a job at the end of the course.

Short, sharp courses can get you working *fast*

If you simply want to boost your skills in a particular area, you could study a relevant unit. For example, Pitman qualifications offer single-subject exams so you can focus on a particular subject. You now have the opportunity to mix and match the courses you want so that you can design a programme that suits your individual career interests and fits in with other things going on in your life, such as a college course, raising a family or working full time. You can study for units such as:

- customer service;
- public relations;
- European studies;
- financial studies;
- legal studies;
- marketing;
- media;
- conference planning and management;
- recruitment and induction of staff;
- selling and sales management;
- import/export;
- travel and tourism.

There are also one-day courses to boost your skills in topics such as Outlook, the Internet, e-mail, Excel, PowerPoint, Access and Publisher and you should be able to find a level to suit your knowledge and ability. There are, for example, three levels of ability for Word, Excel and PowerPoint in the form of basic, intermediate and advanced. Many agencies offer training opportunities, frequently in partnership with private training colleges.

If your keyboarding skills are zilch, there are touch-typing courses you can do – usually with the hours to suit you – so that you'll know how to lay out business letters, be accurate on the keyboard, check your work for accuracy and build up your speed. You'll learn your way round a keyboard and how to look after it, for example that you should not spill your coffee over it or hit the keys too hard when it crashes again for the third time that morning.

Don't forget too that many colleges of further education run 'returning to work' courses designed to boost job-hunting skills for those who have been out of the workplace for a while, perhaps to raise a family. Your local job centre or college will have details of these.

Useful addresses to contact for information are:

The London Chamber of Commerce and Industry Examinations Board
Athena House
112 Station Road

Sidcup
Kent DA15 7BJ
Tel: (020) 8309 3000
www.lccieb.co.uk

OCR (Oxford, Cambridge and Royal Society for Arts Examinations)
1 Regent Street
Cambridge CB2 1GG
Tel: (01223) 552552
www.ocr.org.uk

Pitman Qualifications
1 Giltspur Street
London EC1A 9DD
Tel: (020) 7294 2800
www.city-and-guilds.co.uk

Qualifications will vary according to the sector you want to work in. You can get more details on training to be a medical secretary, farm secretary and legal secretary from these organisations:

Association of Medical Secretaries, Practice Managers, Administrators and Receptionists (AMSPAR)
Tavistock House North
Tavistock Square
London WC1H 9LN
Tel: (020) 7387 6005
www.amspar.co.uk

ILEX (Paralegal Training) Ltd
Kempston Manor
Kempston
Bedford MK42 7AB
Tel: (01234) 841000
www.ilex.org.uk
Runs year-long legal secretary diploma courses in colleges nation-wide plus correspondence courses.

Institute of Agricultural Secretaries and Administrators
NAC
Stoneleigh
Kenilworth
Warwickshire CV8 2LZ
Tel: (0247) 669592
www.iagsa.co.uk

The Institute of Paralegal Training
The Mill
Clymping Street
Clymping
Littlehampton
West Sussex BN17 5RN
Tel: (01903) 714276
www.paralegaltraining.co.uk

You can study through a wide range of methods now, and these include:

▌ open learning, picking things up as you go;
▌ working your way through a structured programme of learning at your own pace when it suits you;
▌ online/CD ROM;
▌ attending classes, for example in the evening, during the weekends, or in the daytime, at a college of further education or an adult education college;
▌ by correspondence;
▌ signing up for a full-time course at a college of further or higher education, university, private training college or centre, or secretarial college;
▌ studying a subject simply to get skilled up in it, for example signing up for an Excel course to become competent in your use of Excel;
▌ learning on the job, by temping or by joining a structured government training programme, such as New Deal or the Modern Apprenticeship scheme.

Places to find information on courses include:

- local careers service companies and school, college and university careers services – they will know what colleges and training centres have to offer in your area; try contacting the Connexions Service at www.connexions.gov.uk, or Careers Wales at www.careerswales.com;
- *Yellow Pages* or www.yell.com, looking under training, education and secretarial training;
- Learn Direct (tel: 0800 900100; Web site: www.learndirect.co.uk) – call or visit their Web site to find the course for you;
- Web sites for hotcourses.com, floodlight.co.uk and ucas.ac.uk – they all provide information on the courses available and offer plenty of advice.

To ensure that your distance learning course is accredited, contact:

Association of British Correspondence Colleges
PO Box 17926
London SW19 3WB
Tel: (020) 8544 9559
www.homestudy.org.uk
This association safeguards the interests of all students taking correspondence courses by ensuring its members deliver a high standard of tuition and service.

Open and Distance Learning Quality Council
16 Park Crescent
London W1B 1AH
Tel: (020) 7612 7090
This body accredits distance learning courses.

If your course is directly related to a particular job, you can apply for a career development loan. Your careers service will have details, or you can visit www.lifelonglearning.co.uk for more information. Your local Learning and Skills Council should also have information. You should be aware that many recruitment agencies have partnerships with training providers to provide CD ROM and online courses, so it's worth visiting their Web site to see if the agency you propose to sign up with has such a facility.

Developing your managerial and social skills

It's important to remember that you don't have to go on a course to develop the skills employers want and PAs need to have. Vacation work, volunteering and temping will teach you a lot about working in teams under pressure and handling people and other transferable musts. If you can market them properly on your CV and spot areas where they'll transfer into the workplace, then you'll have lots of scope for talking about the things you *can* do. For more details of volunteering activities, contact:

Community Service Volunteers (CSV)
237 Pentonville Road
London N1 9NJ
Tel: (020) 7278 6601   www.csv.org.uk

National Centre for Volunteering
Regent's Wharf
8 All Saints Street
London N1 9RL
Tel: (020) 7520 8900   www.volunteering.org.uk

TimeBank
The Mezzanine
Elizabeth House
39 York Road
London SE1 7NQ
Tel: (020) 7401 5420   www.timebank.org.uk

What makes an outstanding PA?

You need technical skills to be a top PA, but there are other qualities you'll need on the job that are just as important if you want to get to the top. These are crucial to busy executives and organisations alike, and include:

- a high level of commercial understanding;
- the ability to manage projects;
- a solid range of IT skills;

- working beyond the job description;
- being committed to the organisation;
- hunger or ambition to get things done;
- flexibility and initiative;
- good judgement calls – 'She knows when to keep quiet';
- somebody who seeks to set the standard for excellence;
- the ability to adapt to constantly changing environments;
- trust – the boss must trust you to see that things get done in good time and that you know what to do and say;
- instant chemistry between PA and boss – you must be able to work closely together for long periods of time.

Some qualities will be more important than others to an employer – all bosses have their own idea of what they want in PAs, which may include:

- taking all the worry off the bosses' shoulders, leaving bosses to focus on the business side of things;
- self-reliance;
- reliability – bosses never having to check that something has been done;
- being a first-class juggler;
- being switched on;
- being proactive – a 'get off your backside and do it' sort of person;
- tons of initiative;
- emotional intelligence;
- competence;
- confidence;
- research capability – the ability to find things out for them-selves;
- an enquiring mind;
- always being one step ahead;
- being professional;
- being politically astute;
- paying great attention to detail;
- staying late without being asked when it's necessary;
- personality;
- intelligence;
- a sense of humour;

- attitude – the can-do approach or the attitude that nothing is too much trouble;
- always going the extra mile;
- willingness to get their hands dirty and join in at the lowest level – no room for prima donnas here;
- accepting only the highest standards;
- working without any supervision;
- willingness to speak up if they think the boss is in the wrong;
- doing hundreds of things that we know nothing about but that they know need to be done.

Most bosses will put more emphasis on one or two qualities and abilities than on others. They all have their 'absolutely must have' on the shopping list when they're looking to recruit a new PA. Some will be very particular to a role and a boss:

- 'Applicant must be a cat lover.'
- 'Must have a head for figures.'
- 'Applicants should be committed Christians.'
- 'The successful candidate will be able to think out of the box.'
- 'Your sense of confidentiality must be irreproachable.'

Inevitably, there will be things that irritate you about each other. But everybody has faults, and what matters is that the basic chemistry is there and you hit it off from the start. Without that good feeling, you're in for a very bumpy ride and will need to be very tenacious and have lots of stickability.

Summary

- Ultimately, when faced with a number of potential employees all with similar backgrounds, the one the boss or team is likely to choose is the one who fits into the culture and values of the organisation most readily.
- Good sound skills, introductory experience and qualifications are the prerequisites to a career as a PA.
- Personal qualities are also of paramount importance – some organisations and bosses put more emphasis on certain qualities than others.

7 Searching out the opportunities

This chapter will help you identify your way into the PA world and find where the jobs are.

Getting information on what you need to know

Remind yourself of the successful ingredients of job hunting in terms of an integral career action plan:

- self-knowledge, so that you know exactly what you want, not just in a job but in your life as well, and so that you can sell your skills and abilities all the more effectively;
- an awareness of the opportunities available and how to secure the right one for you (eg how to write a CV, hunt for the right job, network);
- chemistry with the people you work for – if you're going to work long hours together in a tight-knit team, you need to be able to hit it off.

If you're not sure of where you want to be, some roles offer an excellent opportunity to try out different positions as a float secretary before deciding which one is best for you. In others, you'll spend time in a section or team and be covering for people who are on holiday or off sick, which is still a useful way to find out what life is like elsewhere. Alternatively, a stint of temping will enable you to:

- work in different organisations, so that you can decide what sort of place you want to be in;
- get experience on the job;
- land a job – you could really hit it off with the boss;
- get a reference;
- get cash coming in;
- boost your network of people who can give you work;
- strengthen your skills set – working with different systems all the time quickly enables you to move from one to another and become skilled in using a wide range of applications by picking things up as you go, asking others for help and attending structured courses;
- boost your ability to cope with change, new situations and people;
- acquire a picture of what life is like at the top if you are asked to fill a senior position for a few days – such an experience won't last for ever and will give you an insight into what life is like.

How do you plan to go job hunting?

Not only has the communications and information technology revolution transformed the way we work, but it has totally redrawn the boundaries within which those seeking work can find it. The World Wide Web means you can access information about job vacancies anywhere in the world, and get plenty of advice on CV writing, interview techniques, employment law, courses you might want to take and companies that operate in the sector you want to join. There are different kinds of Web sites you can investigate when you're job hunting, and they are:

- the company Web site/printed careers material;
- recruitment agency sites;
- newspapers that have their own sites;
- general recruitment sites.

Any agencies you go through online should be a member of the Association of Online Recruiters, and you should check that you can cancel any subscriptions you have to pay to register. There should be a telephone number on the Web page – you need to be able to talk to a human being in the event that something goes wrong. The site should have a privacy statement so you know exactly whom your CV and details are going to, and, to protect yourself, you should never give out any work phone number as a contact number – use your mobile. If you decide to go online job hunting, boost your knowledge about the process and become more aware of the pros and cons. Finally, many companies track people who log on to job-hunting Web sites, so don't do it at work!

Visiting companies' Web pages

If you're looking for particular organisations in your locality, you can use the _Yellow Pages_ to find them, either online or in print. Over 3 million companies in the UK have Web sites. Don't forget to visit local government sites, which can provide useful links to their opportunities and any charities in the area.

Visiting a company's Web pages enables you to get a lot of information quickly, including recent press releases and whether or not the company is recruiting (so long as the pages are updated regularly). They can tell you about a company's mission statement, goals and ethics, its history, global reach, products and services, and career opportunities. Check out the management structure – many will have photographs and bibliographies of the people at the top, and it will give you an idea of where support roles might fit into the basic organisation. Try to work out the tone of the site. What impression does it give you of the company? Sociable? Friendly? Professional? Formal? Could you see yourself working with any of the team displayed on it? Whether you're actually applying for a job with a specific company or just want to check out the Web site, you can learn a lot by considering the sort of image the company seeks to portray and how closely that relates to you and your values.

Most have careers, jobs or recruitment pages; some have chat rooms, enabling you to make contact with current employees. At the least, you should be able to e-mail your CV to it if you think it looks like the sort of organisation you would like to work for.

Recruitment agencies

Despite the considerable strides that have been made in terms of recruiting online, many people ultimately prefer the personal approach, dealing with somebody face to face or over the telephone. The recruitment agency is very big business in the UK, worth over £22 billion. Its professional body, which guarantees standards to those who use it, is called the Recruitment and Employment Confederation (REC). It has 8,000 individual members (recruitment consultants and managers) and 6,000 corporate member offices (consultancies and agencies).

Agencies vary in nature, so you'll need to decide which one is right for you. The key factor is to sign up with an agency that is a member of REC. Some are generalist, focusing on many sectors and careers, but having specialist divisions, while others focus solely on one area, such as teachers, nursery nurses or drivers. There are many secretarial agencies about and they pride themselves on their expertise and knowledge of the markets they provide for. Some are known for their focus, such as Part-Time Careers. If you want to join a particular sector, it makes sense to go to where the expertise is. Visit www.recruitment500.com to find a list of secretarial agencies and their focus, although it does concentrate on London. Other agencies have divisions for graduates, or first-time job seekers. Some agencies specialise in the higher end of the market – Angela Mortimer being one, offering a division that recruits exclusively for chief executives, board-level directors, entrepreneurs and chairmen. Some agencies specialise in assisting bilingual PAs, so if you're a linguistic specialist try to find a recruitment agency specialising in bilingual secretarial recruitment. This can be especially helpful if you have a language whose business use isn't as common as say French, German and Spanish, such as Urdu or Hindi.

To find employment agency sites in your local area, visit www.yell.com, enter your postcode or town and the words 'recruitment agency' and you'll have a list of those in your area. Alternatively you can check the printed version of *Yellow Pages* at home or in your public library. Recruitment agencies may be local, regional (based in towns throughout your area), national or international in character. Examples of national agencies include Office Angels at www.office-angels.com, Manpower at www.manpower.co.uk and Reed at www.reed.co.uk.

When you sign up with an agency, you should expect to:

- take your CV along and dress as if you are going for an interview;
- be tested on your IT skills (including speeds), spelling and grammar;
- be questioned about your track record, motivation and career aspirations;
- have a discussion with an adviser who will help you find the sort of role you are looking for, so that you can best be placed with an employer and position that will excite and suit you.

The adviser should:

- help you to determine whether your application should be sent on to an employer for any current vacancies, along with others;
- arrange interviews for you and provide feedback on your performance;
- give you advice on improving your interview technique.

Agencies' staff should interview you in private, away from people coming into their offices off the street, and away from telephones. Importantly, they should be very discreet, with a policy of no names and no numbers left on your desk while you're job hunting. Most have barred phones, so that it's impossible for anyone to use the 1471 system to trace their calls to you.

Agencies try to develop relationships with employers because for one thing it means they can better understand their organisations and how they work, the culture and possible 'fit' required of new recruits. They continually work to improve the service they are providing candidates and clients by doing customer/client satisfaction surveys. All this means that they should be better able to brief you on the organisation itself, and match your needs, motivation and aspirations to companies they think will be interested in recruiting you. It also means that they should be able to brief you more thoroughly on any role you decide to apply for.

Most agencies have Web sites outlining the services they offer and what you can expect if you are a job hunter. Some are linked to training providers, and offer packages enabling you to boost your skills while waiting for the right job to come along. Many run events – informal gatherings with food and drink – designed to help candidates meet each other.

General recruitment sites

Examples of these sites include:

- www.jobsite.co.uk;
- www.totaljobs.com;
- www.workthing.com;
- www.monster.co.uk.

They all offer lots of advice to job hunters with vacancies from a very wide range of careers, including PA/secretarial posts. Many such sites enable you to submit your CV online. Many have a discussion forum and tips for getting the best job.

The press

Local, regional and national newspapers all offer advice on job hunting and trends in the market, with advice columns, and frequently profiles of people working in a sector, to give you an idea of what to expect. Most have Web sites too, with far more jobs on them than they have room for in the printed press. Well-known examples of national papers with supplements include:

- *The Times*: *Crème* on Wednesdays and a small section each Friday; there is a Web site, www.thetimes-appointments. co.uk/sites/creme, that also has information on secretarial events;
- *Guardian*: with *Office World* on Monday and a smaller subsection on Saturday; their Web site is www.jobsunlimited.co.uk;
- *Evening Standard* runs a *Just the Job* section on Mondays, with *Professional Secretary* – check out www.thisislondon.co.uk/jobs;
- *Independent* at www.independent.co.uk.

An alternative is www.fish4.co.uk, a consortium of national and local newspapers enabling you to suss out vacancies in your locality.

There is also a range of recruitment magazines, handed out at mainline London train stations, including _Girl about Town_ (_GAT_), _Ms London_ and _Nine to Five_, and also:

- _Office Secretary Magazine_, published four times a year by Peebles Media Group;
- _Executive PA Magazine_, published four times a year by Hobsons Publishing;
- _Executive Secretary_, published five times a year by Salisbury House Publishing;
- _Executive Woman_ (incorporating the _Businesswoman_);
- _Career Secretary_, published by the Institute of Qualified Private Secretaries for members, quarterly.

Additionally, you shouldn't forget sites such as www.pa-assist.com that have a multitude of useful tips and advice. They will be invaluable to you, not only while you are looking for a job, but also in making the most of it when you have acquired one.

Jobs in the public sector tend to be advertised locally in papers and job centres. The official local government recruitment Web site, www.lgjobs.com, has advice on applying and career profiles. Other useful places to look for information about working in the public sector include:

Local Government Opportunities
Local Government Training Organisation
Layden House
76–86 Turnmill Street
Farringdon
London EC1M 5QU
Tel: (020) 7296 6503
www.lgcareers.com

NHS Careers
PO Box 376
Bristol BS99 3EY
Tel: 0845 60 60 655
www.nhscareers.nhs.uk

Working for a Charity
The Peel Centre
Perry Circus
London WC1X 9EY
Tel: (020) 7833 8220
www.wfac.org.uk

Visit www.jobsplus@charityconnections.co.uk and www.jobs4 publicsector.com, useful Web sites if you wish to work in either sector.

Networking

The cost of recruiting the wrong person cannot be over-estimated. Consequently, recruitment is not so much about what you know as whom you know. Some 70 per cent of jobs are filled not through advertising at all but simply by recruiting people known to the organisation. Many employers prefer to recruit by taking on people who are 'tried and tested' with them, who know how the company works and what its ethos is – and who have shown they are a good fit with the rest of the team, perhaps by working first as a temp. Others take people on through the recommendation of friends and contacts. The more people you know in the industry or sector, the greater your chances of picking up a job. In fact, some organisations pay a fee to staff who recommend individuals to them, where those people are taken on successfully.

Being in the right place at the right time: temping

You can land your dream job simply by being in the right place at the right time and hitting it off with your prospective boss. That's how a number of successful partnerships start out. If you propose to land a job by temping, choose the agency you sign up with carefully to increase your chances of working in the right sector. Agencies who specialise in an area, such as media or the arts, will give you sound advice about 'getting in' and the companies they deal with in their area. If you can't get into your chosen field right away, look for something related to it to gain experience in that. If you can get in as a temp, you're in a strong position to make an impact and establish a reputation for yourself, so it's important to raise your profile within the company and show what you can do.

If you can 'get in' with a company, you may be able to work there for a long time and circle around different departments. People always want good cover and they are always reassured by having someone who's been recommended to them. You can also make yourself indispensable by learning company procedures and 'who's who' within the organisation, so that you can easily switch from one desk to another.

As you network, you'll build a solid list of contacts who can help you find the job you want. Find out who has the power to recruit support staff. Identify those who make the decisions about hiring and firing and get to know them. If professionals see somebody who is good, these days they will want to hang on to them. But unless you tell people you're interested in staying, they won't know.

In most companies, those with the power to recruit are now bosses, supervisors, or section or business unit heads, the ones who'll be spending the day alongside prospective recruits. These are the people who can send a strong message to HR or the office manager that they like a person, think the person is good and want to keep him or her. If you want to join a company, say in the marketing area, give your CV to the head of that area as opposed to human resources. Marketing know exactly what they need and

109

are looking for in new recruits. HR personnel are a step away and don't talk quite the same language. You can, of course, also approach the human resources professionals, who organise the entire recruiting process from promoting the need for staff to checking references, and talk to them about career opportunities in the company.

Research all the avenues of information open to you to see where future opportunities might lie. Check staff noticeboards and the company intranet, if there is one, for details of current vacancies. Stop by the HR department and try to have 10 to 15 minutes with a member of staff there to drop your CV off. Find out about the company's recruiting practices. Does it pick up people full time who have had work experience for them or are employed as temps? Don't be afraid to be pushy, but be polite. If you want to talk to your boss or supervisor about future opportunities, ask for five minutes with that person privately and give an indication of what it's about. Remember that companies want to hold on to good people. If you're doing well, they'll want to hold on to you and they'll find a way to do it. If you want to stay on, take action and tell the right people.

Develop a network of contacts within the company. Get to know who's who. Keep a list of people you meet, and attend social events if you're given the opportunity to go – and introduce yourself! Show an interest in people and their companies. Tell people what you do and show enthusiasm for it. Many people may want someone to do a one-off project for them at home, such as setting up a computer program. Meet people outside the company. Go to bars where people who work in the same industry are. Most people know of someone who is recruiting. You may find out about small businesses that simply want extra help for a few hours. Go to any secretarial and careers events where you will have the opportunity to meet employers and make new contacts.

The benefits of joining a professional organisation, such as the Institute of Qualified Private Secretaries (see Chapter 11, 'Useful addresses'), is that you can make contacts with people in a wide circle of sectors and at different levels. It was formed in 1957 and runs conferences, seminars and meetings, all designed to encourage a free exchange of ideas, opinions and experiences. There's a quarterly journal, *Career Secretary*. It has some 2,500 members and gives you a chance to make your mark and prove what you can do in professional events and projects nationally and locally. It has 13 regional branches in many areas of the UK. It may be able to help you get a foot in the door, as you meet people who'll keep your name in mind when positions come up.

Summary

'What can I do to increase my chances of landing the job I want?'

- Think about what's right for you.
- Do your homework – check out the organisations you want to join.
- Get related experience (eg if you're looking to work in the non-profit sector, it would help to show you've done volunteer work, preferably in the area you plan to work in – show you can relate to your customers).
- Get to know the right people in your company.
- Network, and tell people what you want.
- Show what you can do, not just in this current job but outside it too.
- Use action words in your CV.
- Show a passion for what you're doing and work well.
- Raise your profile and portray the right image, interested and passionate about what's happening.
- Acquire a reputation as somebody who is competent with a can-do approach and attitude.

8 *Landing that role*

This chapter will help you sell yourself and hopefully land an interview and then a job!

Writing your CV

The purpose of writing a CV is to get an interview. But before you start putting pen to paper or fingers to keyboard, remember that recruiters are seriously busy people. They don't have time to spend hours labouring over CVs, and it may take some recruiters as little as 20 seconds to decide whether your CV goes to the 'interview', 'reserve' or 'reject' pile. Some CVs won't even get to the reject pile but find themselves dumped straight into the waste-paper basket. These are usually the ones containing spelling or grammatical errors, coffee stains, grubby paw marks and gimmicks. So read up on how to write a CV before you start writing yours. Your public library and careers service and any bookshop will have plenty of useful books, and many agencies have Web sites with advice on writing a CV. But basic golden rules to follow are:

- Keep your CV short – two pages of A4 is enough. Your CV should entice the employer to want to meet you to find out more.
- Put your contact details on the top of page one, with your e-mail address and mobile number if you have them; and your name at the top of the other pages, in case the pages all become detached from each other.

- Include a personal summary at the top: three or four lines outlining the sort of person you are and the role you want.
- Be relevant. Prospective employers want to know what makes you tick *now*. Show them you want to do the job, and that you have the skills, the experience and, if necessary, the qualifications to do the job.
- Be honest. Many employers use validators to run a comprehensive check on your claims to qualifications and experience.
- If you name referees in your application, make sure they're willing to write a reference for you. Outline the job to them and give them a copy of your CV. It will help them to write a more useful reference.
- Use plain, white A4 paper, and a plain, white A4 envelope if you're sending the application by post. Send it first class – or by e-mail.
- Spell out specific skills and knowledge you've learnt through courses you've studied. Don't leave employers to guess what course abbreviations stand for.
- Make sure the CV's layout is easy to follow and read. Keep it in a Word document if you're sending it by e-mail (unless otherwise specified). Use heading and bullet points, as opposed to paragraphs of prose.
- Re-produce your CV for every new job you apply for, reflecting any terminology used in adverts, such as human resources rather than personnel if that's what they use.
- Make your CV easy to photocopy.

Show the employer the sort of person you are. Employers want 'well-rounded, motivated people', not couch potatoes. Many like to see voluntary work on a CV – it shows them what motivates and drives you. Give them an idea of the contribution you've made to previous teams, be they in a work situation or voluntary effort, or at school or college. Don't be bashful – if you don't blow your own trumpet, nobody else will. *Show* you've got energy and initiative by using action-packed words that display your get-up-and-go approach, such as:

- trained;
- mentored;

- controlled;
- improved;
- researched;
- managed;
- recruited;
- coached;
- developed;
- established;
- organised;
- reduced.

Expand on these verbs, eg 'trained new staff on procedures'. Add weight to your CV by adding numbers (eg 75 words per minute), percentages, monetary values and so on, because employers can relate to this information.

Case study: Show them you've got a can-do approach
Susan, PA in media

I got my job because I'm good at organising things and I'm a good team player. On my CV, one of my points was: 'Established successful women's cricket club at university. Raised over £3,000 for the local hospice by playing five matches against local teams in one season. Won three out of the five.' When I went for interview, they used my CV to pick up on all the things I'd done, like starting the women's cricket club. We talked about the importance of working as a team, and because I'd done quite a lot of this I could talk about problems we'd met and how we'd overcome them, and my role in a team. I could talk about what I'd achieved. You have to have confidence in your own abilities, however small they are at first. I mean, if you're leaving school and going straight out into your first job, you'd have a very different range of experiences to draw on than if you were a graduate, and employers know that.

Your CV can show employers the sort of person you are and the role you like to play in a team. Highlight your job-specific skills, such as Microsoft Word, on your CV, with the languages as a bonus. E-mail your CV and you'll show you've got technical skills right from the outset, and, importantly, that you're confident using the e-mail system. Be honest about your language abilities on your CV, because you may be tested at interview. Don't list too many hobbies and interests in your CV, or the employer reading it will wonder if you have any time or energy left for work.

Write a well-thought-out covering letter or e-mail to accompany your CV. Explain why you're interested in the role, if you have a specific one in mind, but if there isn't then outline where you are now and where you want to be. Give contact numbers – home and mobile but *not* any workplace you're employed at – in the covering letter or e-mail.

Finally, always copy anything you send to employers or agencies, be it by fax, e-mail or snail mail. You can refresh your memory by rereading what you put before your interview.

Forming that personal relationship: the interview

So you've been asked for an interview – congratulate yourself. The company, or more specifically the team or boss you'd be working with, wants to meet you and find out more about what you can do for them. Crucially they want to assess how well you'd fit into the team you'd be working with and the overall culture of the organisation. However interviews are conducted, it's important to remember that they are a two-way process. It's essential that you find out exactly what role the employer has in mind for you and how flexible they are about what you might do above and beyond that. You also need to think whether you all hit it off and whether you would work well together. If you are going to be working for a team, you're more likely to be interviewed by various members of that team and also any other secretaries you'll be working with.

Find out what you can about your future employer before you get there – don't rely on others to brief you. Show the interviewers why the company is your preferred choice. Be able to explain what interests you about the sector. If you're a graduate and going into a business environment, try to show that you follow the business pages in serious papers such as *The Times*, the *Financial Times* and the *Wall Street Journal*. Show that you know what the key issues are in the sector, and current developments and trends. If you're going to apply for a job in a specialist department, such as human resources or IT, try to show an understanding for what these functions do and how they support the business. Tell them about relevant experiences that show you know what you're letting yourself in for.

Do your homework:

- Check out the organisation's Web site.
- Read any career brochures available.
- Check out any press articles – what the company's in the news for (assuming it's good news).
- Visit a showroom if they have one.
- Read the annual report or at least look at it.
- Remind yourself what your unique selling points are that make you different and set you apart from the other candidates.
- Think up examples of times you've used the skills this employer wants.

Practical musts include arriving 10 minutes early to give yourself time to freshen up. If you're really nervous, walk for 10 minutes to work off excess energy before you go in. Be polite to every single person you meet – they may be asked what they thought of you after you leave. After all, if you land the job, you'll be working with them. Finally, switch your mobile phone off.

Prepare mentally, too, for requests for information and questions you might be asked, such as:

- What are your strengths?
- Tell us about yourself.
- What are your weaknesses?
- Where do you see yourself in five years' time?
- What is your proudest achievement?

- Why should we select you over any other candidate? What are your unique selling points?
- Tell us about your career so far. Why did you choose the jobs you've chosen to do?
- Which other jobs are you applying for and why?
- What have you found out about…?
- Tell us about a situation where you…
- Is there anything else you'd like to ask us? (If questions have been covered, say so.)
- Is there anything else we should know about you? (Try to finish with a closing statement outlining three to five key points you can bring to the role and the organisation – your unique selling points.)
- A killer question such as 'Tell me a joke' or 'What question are you dreading I'll ask at this interview?' to show you can think on your feet.

From your point of view, it's important to think of questions to ask at interview, so that you're in a strong position to make an informed decision about the job if it is offered to you. Try to show you've given thought to the sort of role you want and get an idea for how the organisation treats PAs and support staff.

Choosing the right boss

I have mentioned several times already that PAs must be able to handle people well in order to do their jobs successfully. The relationship between a PA and the boss (or chief boss) is so close that it's like a successful marriage. You can tell how close people get to their bosses when three out of four PAs in one office admitted to calling their boss 'darling' by mistake! PAs and bosses get to know each other's thoughts, what the other person will want next, what sort of mood the other is in without asking and how to cheer him or her up when things aren't going so well. Central to the success of the role of PA is the relationship between the PA and the boss or bosses. Will they click or not? Will they want to spend long hours working together? Gut instinct when you meet for the first time will tell you a great deal.

Bosses differ. Some are approachable, with a great sense of humour, fair and appreciative. They believe in life after 5. Others are fast and dynamic, some slow and measured and fussy. Others have a hot temper. They may be control freaks, and irritating with it: you'll arrange something and then they have to change something ever so slightly (and unnecessarily) just to assert themselves and feel as though they are in control. Some manage with fairly limited support, because they're independent. They may expect you to have a degree in mind-reading, which can create problems, because they never see why they should tell you where they're going, so you spend half your time trying to find them. Others need to have their hand held throughout the day, either because they need to be looked after or because they are so busy they need somebody else to do the practical thinking for them. Some are great at keeping to time – whereas others will have blown your carefully prepared schedule for the day within the first hour, as their first meeting runs an hour over time. Others will make promises to people without any thought of the practicalities of what they are saying they'll do, creating havoc for those who have to come along behind and clear up the mess and meet the promise. Then you have the whirlwinds, rarely in the office, but leaving it like a tornado's been through when they do make an appearance.

All bosses have their good and bad points, and one way to find out whether they have a history of being difficult is to find out how many secretaries they have had in the last few years. If they've been through a few, that should be telling you something. Some people will see this as a challenge: 'I bet I'll be able to handle this boss'; others will take the hint and move on fast.

What do people look for in a boss? Key qualities may include:

- flexibility;
- sense of humour;
- good communication;
- being approachable;
- giving positive feedback;
- being well organised;
- being supportive;
- fairness;

▓ willingness to give you responsibility;
▓ keeping you informed;
▓ valuing you as more of a partner than a PA;
▓ not giving you mounds of work to do at 5 o'clock (which 'is urgent and must go out tonight') and then going off to a meeting and failing to return.

Trust and respect between you and the boss are essential if the relationship is going to work well, as high-level assistants are increasingly given responsibility for company decisions and you'll handle the people who are most important to the boss: those he or she loves, such as partner, kids and friends; and those his or her business and professional image relies on to survive, such as clients and colleagues.

What will the role actually involve?

Some PAs do still play the traditional role, which includes tasks such as sewing on buttons and making the tea, so if you don't want this sort of role grill those you'll be working with carefully, but without making yourself out to be a prima donna who won't muck in. Questions you might ask both the boss and the current PA, if there is one (because if they have different answers, it will be telling you something right from the start), are:

▓ What does the job description cover (ie what are the basics)?
▓ What role does the boss have in the organisation and how is it changing? This will give you a feel for what the boss does and how your role will be affected.
▓ What does the boss expect from the PA? What qualities are on the 'must have' and 'must not have' lists?
▓ Why did the current PA take the job? Why is the current PA leaving and what is he or she going on to (so that you can get a feel for whether the person is going on to bigger and better things)?
▓ How has the current PA's role expanded and changed during the employment and how much of that was self-driven?
▓ How much real control will you have over the diary?

▌ Will you have any projects to manage? If not, what scope is there for getting into project work? Are there any in the pipeline?

▌ How much autonomy will you have? How could you develop the role so you have more?

▌ What are the boss's faults and weaknesses in managing a group? And what are the boss's pet hates in PAs?

▌ Ask the boss to describe a typical working day or week. Get a feel for how much of it is dedicated to the organisation, to charity and to personal life.

Ask about the organisation:

▌ How are the goals of the organisation communicated to staff and how often?

▌ What central support services exist, such as photocopying, mail room, couriers, catering staff, corporate relations, presentation operators? (This will give you an idea of what sort of support you can expect and what you might end up doing all day.)

▌ How much has the company restructured in the last two years? Five years? Is one due? This will give you an idea for how much your role could change in the future, if a restructuring is imminent or long overdue, and how responsive the organisation is to change.

▌ What happens when other PAs are ill or on holiday? Do temps come in, or are you expected to cover for each other?

▌ How many telephones will you have to 'cover'? (This will give you an idea of whether your role is likely to be that of a glorified receptionist.)

Try to talk to more than one secretary to suss out how roles within the organisation may differ. You'll get an idea for how you'd fit in with your new colleagues. Would you look forward to seeing them and working with them on a Monday morning? Could you envisage sitting beside them all day?

A key point that many consider to be as important as any perk is that of career and personal development. This is a difficult one to gauge, because many companies promise it but the reality is that they don't practise what they preach. Much comes down to the basic enthusiasm of your new bosses as to whether they actually *want* you to progress at all. It may not suit them if you come in bursting with enthusiasm for this idea you thought up at 4 o'clock in the morning. Try to find out whether the organisation takes up ideas from the support staff or seeks to 'keep them in their place' with a glass ceiling. What scope is there for the senior PA? Try to get an idea of what the next role after the one you land might be. If you're joining a large organisation, find out what structure exists for the staff in terms of promotion. What happens to the executive secretaries once they have been at this level for two, three or four years? Are they destined to stay where they are, or can they move on into something else? If the former, you may need to move on to another organisation at that point.

Find out from other support staff how their careers have developed. Do they have regular appraisals? Has the post given them new skills, knowledge, feelings of self-worth, and self-confidence, and if so how have they achieved this? Have they gone on courses or taught themselves? And who has been the enthusiast for this development? The assistant, company and/or boss, or all three? This will show you how driven (and motivated and enthusiastic) your new colleagues are likely to be. Some people are always more ambitious than others, but it's important to suss out what emphasis the organisation puts on personal and career development for its PAs, and how important your prospective colleagues deem it to be, never mind the professionals.

How much bureaucracy can you take?

Generally, the larger the organisation is, the greater is the amount of bureaucracy so that management can keep an eye on spending costs – and so the greater is the element of control there's likely to be. Try to get an idea of how bureaucratic a firm is because that's the sort of thing that people either cope with well and don't mind blowing their way through or can't stand and tire of quickly. If you have no choice but to handle bureaucracy, and it turns out to be the one sore point about the company, then the way to handle it is to deal with those matters as fast as you can – make it a game with yourself to turn such matters around faster every time you do them, so that you can get on with the more interesting stuff.

Match the process and procedure to the task in hand so that you get a good idea of what you'll need to go through to get anything done. Find out how long it takes to get things signed off, how many people need to sign off on them and what happens when they're not around. Dig deep for answers. Then, if you take the job there won't be any surprises.

How flexible are you prepared to be?

PAs must be flexible, ready and willing to turn their hand to anything. Most of us would say yes, of course we are – but the reality is that we're not as flexible as we think. Would you:

- lie for the boss?
- stay late regularly?
- look after the boss's kids for a morning?
- walk the boss's dog?
- organise shooting parties for the boss?

We all have our own limits. Work out what is within your remit and code of ethics, and be prepared to say so if you're asked to do something that goes beyond them. It's no good thinking about this sort of thing after you've been offered the job because by then you could be landed with tasks like walking the Rottweiler twice a day in all weathers. Find out what the boss's personal interests are so that you can get an idea for what you might be handling and the sort of people who will be calling. If you're applying to work for somebody who needs you to organise his or her whole life, you can't sidestep these sorts of tasks.

And after the interview: will there be more testing?

How will you be assessed? In large organisations, interviewers may have feedback forms with which to rank your skills, experience and personal qualities on a 1 to 5 scale, giving marks for predetermined skills and abilities they particularly want from candidates. In smaller companies, this is usually less defined and more relaxed. Employers are trying to balance the emotional (will your personality fit in?) with the practical (will you be able to do the job well?) so they may put you through your paces. There's more to the selection procedure than the interview, although if you've gone through an agency most employers will rely on that agency to test your word-processing abilities and even spelling. Some employers will include as part of the selection process some or all of the following:

- a medical;
- getting references;
- checking with validators that all the details you've given on your CV are correct;
- psychometric testing – literacy, numeracy and non-verbal reasoning;
- workplace simulation – giving the employer the chance to test any particular traits they want in successful recruits, such as accuracy and flexibility;
- personality tests to see what your weaknesses and strengths are;
- handwriting;
- presentations;
- specialist skills, such as a PowerPoint presentation.

Every individual is unique and so it's important throughout the whole process to present your unique selling points. They will give the interviewers something to remember you by. Show too how you can add value above and beyond the basic job description.

Feeling young again

If you are moving back into the job market, or are an older job seeker, age discrimination can be a worry. There are things you can do to make yourself youthful and these include:

- Check your image – could a new hairstyle and colouring give you a more youthful appearance?

▌ Emphasise your experience and your ability to hit the ground running.

▌ Show you can work across the ages – if you can mention any activities you do with young people (but *not* your grand-children), so much the better. Show that you relate well to young people.

▌ Upgrade your skills and show you're a firm believer in lifelong learning and that you embrace it.

▌ Learn from young people, their hopes and aspirations and fears for the future.

▌ Show what you can achieve and get done.

▌ Go with agencies that actively focus on the older job seeker, such as Wrinklies Direct (tel: 0870 600 1921) or Forties People (tel: 020 7329 4044), which employers will approach because they want more mature members of staff.

Many employers like mature workers, because they bring to the workplace experience, a sense of responsibility, resilience and excellent levels of numeracy and literacy. They are loyal, enthusiastic and keen to learn skills required today in work. Some areas such as e-commerce like to take on older PAs because the voice of experience over the telephone and in dealings with customers gives weight to the company.

Knowing what you want

Remind yourself before the interview what you want, what you can contribute and what's important to you in an organisation you work for. Go back through your entire application to remind yourself what you told the organisation and try to think of questions they might ask about points on it. Visit their Web site for any press releases and news pertaining to them and to refresh your memory of it, so that you can show interest.

When you come out of the selection process, remind yourself of these points again. If you conclude the employer isn't right for you because there is a gap between what you consider essential and what the employer can offer, call a halt to going any further. If, however, the job contains most of the things you are after, see if you can compromise about the things it's missing. Are there things that make up for the gaps? If there are, then proceed. Weigh up the pros and cons. Listen to your gut instinct and what it's telling you.

Don't waste energy applying to hundreds of thousands of jobs. Be specific about what you want. Wait for the right opportunity to come your way. Use temporary work to get your feet in the door. Show you're serious about your career plans. Show focus, direction and career ambition. People who say 'Oh, I've applied to hundreds of jobs' are sending out the message that they don't really care about what they do.

What is going to clinch the job for you?

Everybody has their special something that will make them sit up and say, 'Yes, this is the job and the company for me.' This could include factors such as:

- stunning offices in the right location;
- chemistry with your prospective boss/es – you hit it off right away and come away thinking, 'Yes, I can see myself working for this boss/team all week';
- the role you think you can develop;
- the opportunity to earn a huge amount of money (how long will this last and how quickly will the meaning of earning money enable you to keep pace with the drudgery of the job itself?);
- how realistic career progression is within the company;
- promises of lots of autonomy and responsibility from day one;
- that gut feeling it's right.

You may have a couple of job offers in hand. Weigh up the right one for you. If you don't have a strong gut feeling towards one as opposed to the other, it may help to write down what you like about each job and what you don't. Don't just consider which job has the most 'likes' and 'dislikes' – look at what those 'likes' and 'dislikes' are, because some are more important than others. Nor should you base the entire decision on the salary offered to you – other perks and elements of the job are important too.

125

Am I going to be paid enough?

At the end of the day, a good salary alone does not a happy employee make. Most of us want a good starting salary, but it's important to look at the overall package. The base sum may not look like much, particularly in many charity and non-profit organisations, but when you add all the perks together things may start to look different.

Perks may include:

- season ticket loan;
- health insurance;
- life assurance;
- pension scheme;
- holiday allowance;
- subsidised gym;
- heath club membership;
- training/study leave;
- career break;
- testing new products;
- profit-related bonus;
- share options;
- staff discounts;
- subsidised cafeteria;
- flexitime;
- free company car parking;
- company product discounts;
- career development.

If the company you join offers perks like these, then they could boost your initial base salary quite a bit, or enhance your lifestyle (through flexitime, for example).

Don't just think about the starting salary. Try to find out when joining a company what the salary could be after you've proved yourself. Will there be a salary review after you've been there for say three months? How often is the salary reviewed thereafter? What affects any rises? Find out whether salary is enhanced by bonuses and, if so, what range of bonuses is commonly given to support staff, and how often? How are bonuses worked out? What are they dependent on? Bonuses may depend on the company's performance over the course or a year, and/or your own showing.

At the end of the day, weigh up what's important to you in terms of what you were looking for in the job from the beginning. How closely do the job you're being offered and the organisation match your values and needs in terms of the challenges, responsibilities, autonomy and variety of the job on the one hand; and the people you'll be working with, the organisation and what it stands for, and the package on the other? Think about that and make your decision.

Summary

▓ Show a professional approach in your job hunting – always do your homework and look after your image.
▓ Think carefully about what you want to achieve in a job.
▓ Listen to your gut instinct and what it is telling you.
▓ Think long term. Where could this role lead?

9 *Excelling at what you do*

Earn the respect of others

One of the first things you need to do is to earn the respect of those around you and form effective working relationships with those you'll be working with. You also need to establish yourself in your own right in the company and in your role. You can do this by a combination of methods: by being totally professional 100 per cent of the time, portraying the right image and working smart, so that you are organised and make the best use of your time. Seek to exceed others' expectations all the time. Raise your profile internally and in terms of anyone you deal with outside the company, and handle good and not-so-good feedback calmly. Finally, it's important to move with the times and accept change well. If you have a clear understanding of what your role is in the company, all this will be easier to achieve.

Be sure of your role and that of those you work for

When you start out in a new role, it takes time to find your feet, especially if you are totally new to the company. You'll need to find out:

- how your new boss works;
- how you can best work effectively together as a team;
- the best way to communicate – probably a combination of voice-mail messages, e-mails and face-to-face meetings;

- company policies and procedures if you're new to the company;
- the suppliers and services your company uses;
- what causes any problems between you and your new team;
- more about your boss's and/or team's role in the organisation;
- who is important in your boss's life and get to know them.

It takes time to pick all this up, and if you have the chance to have a handover with the PA who was there before you then you can cut your learning curve down substantially. You'll also find yourself getting to know your boss as a person: what makes the boss angry, times he or she is best left alone, when it's a good time to talk about your holidays and pay rises. Try to learn about the boss as a person as much as a boss.

You need to be very sure of what your role involves in the big picture: where you and your boss(es) fit into the wheel of the organisation. It can take time to establish a good rapport between you. Talk to your boss about his role and annual goals, so that you can help achieve those. Build up a clear understanding of your organisation's mission, so that you can contribute most effectively to it. And make sure your boss is fully aware of your capabilities and skills set. See how much of the load you can take off the boss or team, especially once you've settled into the role. (Your appraisal provides an excellent opportunity to talk to your boss in detail about this.)

Act and think like a professional

Top PAs take pride in everything they do by setting high standards for themselves (and for others) in the way they behave, project themselves, and handle people and situations. Set yourself high standards in every aspect of your work. Treat others as you would like to be treated yourself. Establish strong working relationships with everybody you come across and work to maintain the good-will between you:

- Take ownership of problems. Sort them yourself if you can. If you can't, try to come up with possible solutions so that you work through the process of coming up with the answers.

Present the one you think best to your boss. Ask how the boss comes up with a solution and why he or she chose it. Learn from the problem-solving process.

- Learn to say no assertively, or delegate.
- Put the client or customer first.
- Be flexible – be willing to stay late where necessary to get the job done.
- Keep your cool when dealing with a difficult person; if you think you're going to lose your temper, count to 10.
- Give yourself a timescale when handling tasks. Aim to do them well within it. Always do what you say you will.
- Set and stick to your own standards, and it becomes second nature to stick to them. If your standards fall at work, people notice.
- Think of 'us' and 'our organisation' and 'our clients' as opposed to 'me' and 'I'. At the end of the day, you're all in it together. At those times when your boss is driving you mad, remember you're on the same side.
- Be honest – always admit if you've made a mistake and apologise.
- Think ahead. Think about where you want to be in one year and five years. Take control of your career, rather than leaving it to stagnate or, worse, to be pushed about by others.

Set yourself high standards

Don't ever let your standards drop. Show you care about what you're doing and your organisation. At the same time, offer to help those who are new, or have less experience – be a coach and mentor to them without acquiring the title. This is particularly the case with IT. The more those you work for can handle themselves, the less IT they will have to hand over to you. Show them short cuts on their PCs and how to learn the fax machine. Apart from anything else, it will make them look good and up to date in the eyes of their peers.

Check things went well if you've organised something or set it up. If things went badly, find out why. Listen without interrupting or jumping in to defend yourself. If you made a mistake, say so and openly apologise. We all make mistakes – we're only human. What matters is the way we put things right and apologise and show that we appreciate things like this matter, and the steps we take to make sure that things don't go wrong again. Get into the habit of appraising yourself constantly. And aim for 100 per cent performance every time. Aim to stand out above everybody else, to be the best.

Know what's going on, both politically in your organisation and outside it in the sector you work in. Be firmly in control – get as much detail as you can.

Case study: There's far more control now than ever before

Sam, PA in a shipping company

Generally, the more you can dot the 'i's' and cross the 't's' the better. It may mean being as specific as telling the boss which floor his meeting with a client is on in a building. If you can find that out in advance of the meeting, you'll save your boss valuable minutes. If I'm organising a meeting, I always confirm the details of meetings by e-mail, with the names of attendees, titles and the organisation they are from; the venue; the day, date and time of the meeting and expected length; the subject; and the contact details of the coordinator in case something needs to be changed. It's important to check out the 'what if' scenario all the time, so that you have a plan B.

I think if you're doing the job properly you acquire tremendous control over your boss's life. I know where my boss is every minute of the day, and how to reach him. That element of control has become so much more important because of the urgency of everything. I've got a file at home with all the crucial phone numbers I need there, in case my boss suddenly needs me at the weekend. I make all his personal appointments – the doctor, hairdresser, fitness trainer – because then I know where he is, and my job is easier. You can handle calls appropriately.

Everything is more detailed than it used to be, because detail helps people identify instantly how urgent something is. Even if you're just taking a telephone message, you can learn a lot. I always find out what the caller wants to speak to my boss about and how time-sensitive it is, when the caller will be available and, as most people have a mobile as well as an office number, which is the best number to reach him or her on to increase the chances of the two hooking up and not playing telephone tag. Then I note down the time and day of the call. All this takes less than a minute, but in a few seconds I have acquired a lot of knowledge and so has my boss.

Confidentiality is important, too, not just in the surrounds of the office in terms of how you store information, but outside it. PAs have to handle a lot of confidential information discreetly and appropriately, even to the point of ensuring it is locked away at night safely, and recognise that there are professional regulations governing this sort of housekeeping.

Portray the right image

PAs who are serious about their career and where it is heading take care to portray the right image. Think about the image you portray, in terms of your appearance, your manners and behaviour, body language and your workstation. Do they resemble somebody who cares about his or her image and job? Have control of all of these areas and you'll work far more effectively.

Remember that, when people come into contact with you, 65 per cent of their image of you will be visual – the way you appear; 30 per cent will be vocal – how you talk and what you say; and 5 per cent will relate to the impact of the content of what you say. If they cannot see you because you are talking on the telephone, then about 70 per cent of their impression of you will be on how you talk; and 30 per cent or so will be on what you say. So smile when you answer the telephone. It really does make a difference.

These points will help you portray the right image:

▓ *Immaculate presentation skills are vital.* You're representing the company as much as anybody else, so think of yourself as an ambassador and fly the flag for your employer. Be loyal to the company at all times. Appearance is important. Check your wardrobe periodically and chuck out anything that is past its sell-by date or you know you have absolutely no hope of getting into any more. Look at those who are in the positions you aspire to. Emulate their dress sense. If you want to join the ranks of management, dress like management, not like somebody from the typing pool. You'll have far more clout. If your company operates a dress-down day, have business attire to hand in case a client drops in – don't get caught out.

▓ *Watch your body language.* Look as if you are listening to what people are saying. You can do this by nodding your head and saying, 'Yes, I see', at appropriate intervals, or asking them if you can check your understanding of what they're saying by repeating it back to them in a different manner. Keep your hands fairly still – don't wave them about too much. Stand up straight and tall – don't slouch at your desk, looking as if you've had too much wine at lunchtime. Above all, don't forget to make eye contact with those you're talking to and to smile!

▓ *Look at your desk.* What does it look like? Does the state of it resemble a minefield of confusion, and force you to spend ages searching for the post-it note you wrote that important number on? Or does it look as if you're organised and clear about what it is that you need to do? Have an organised desk and you'll save time searching for things – and people will have more confidence in your ability to get things done. Ensure your workstation looks professional, even to the point of things you put on the wall around you.

▓ *Check all correspondence whether by e-mail or snail mail before it goes out.* Check:
   – the grammar;
   – the spelling;
   – the tone of the letter;
   – its relevance to the matter in hand;
   – whether it has your direct line at the end.

If you're sending something by e-mail, check whom you're sending it to before you press the send button. If you're

133

sending out an e-mail with dial-in details for a conference call, it may be useful to double-check the dial-in number before you push the send button. And check whether the e-mail has your name at the bottom with your phone number and other contact details.

Case study: When you go on holiday, show you care about your role

Esther, PA in law

It's important to make life easier for everybody when you're on holiday, whether you've got a temp coming in or not. I think it's essential to keep things running as smoothly as you can while you're basking in the sun. I leave some notes about the way I organise my computer and I leave my passwords for the PC and voice-mail. I also leave the names of important clients and people in the company who might call in. I send an e-mail around to tell people that I'll be on holiday, and if there's someone coming in to cover, I give out the name. I always try to do a handover – it does make a difference. I also check that any security passes the temp will need are ready at reception when he or she arrives on their first day; and clear my desk as much as I can when I leave the office. Finally, I always try to call them during the first day to answer any questions they may have before I well and truly leave the office behind. Do I leave contact details of where the office can reach me? Yes. Absolutely.

Work smart

Time is one of the most valuable resources you have. You play a key role in managing your boss's time, filtering information and queries before they reach him or her and trying to handle them yourself – so why not your own?

Look at your week. How much time in and out of work do you spend:

- gossiping on the phone or by e-mail?
- allowing people to interrupt you?
- watching television?
- being hung-over?
- shopping for things you don't really need because you're bored?
- moaning about life?
- worrying?
- thinking about things instead of doing them?
- being disorganised?
- being unfocused on what you want to achieve?

Because we're all human, there are probably things on this list we're all guilty of. Take inspiration from Thomas Edison's words: 'There's a better way to do it – find it.' Apply them to your daily working life and work smart. Routine, tedious jobs will take less time, leaving more time for the exciting stuff. Here are 10 ways to work smart and fit more into your day:

1. Develop your memory for numbers you use frequently. It will save you time looking them up.
2. Go against the clock to get routine tasks done – see how quickly you can do them.
3. Get everything right first time so you don't waste time correcting errors.
4. Increase your typing speed so that you can cover ground more quickly.
5. Never touch the same piece of paper twice: bin it, file it, action it, delegate it – but don't touch it twice.
6. Do the most important tasks when you're at your peak.
7. Set yourself clear goals at the start of each day, week, month and year and then work out how you're going to fit those in.
8. Learn all the short cuts you can on your computer to save you time.
9. Learn how to deal with time wasters and interruptions, and be conscious of how you might waste time.
10. Learn from the methods others use to tackle their workload.

Most captains of industry make use of every minute of the day to expand their knowledge, build their contacts and have the sort of life they want. Can you imagine them wasting their time? Watch those at the top of their company. Look at the way they conduct themselves and their lives. They are very focused on what they want to achieve. They have plenty of energy and motivation. What drives successful people to succeed? Be inspired by them – ask them if you meet them; read about them. Take lessons from their success and focus, and apply them to yourself.

But – because we're all human – learn how to handle procrastination

We all do it. There's that pile you're saving for a rainy day when there is absolutely nothing else to do but go through the pile of stuff you've been putting off for months. Set a time limit and see how much you can get through. And once you've cleared that pile, save yourself the hassle of doing it again six months down the line and adopt the do-it-now approach. Life will be much easier.

Promoting/handling change

Jobs must continue to evolve to keep up with change. Companies have to change constantly to cope with customer demands and social trends, which shift all the time, and to make better use of resources. It's easy to get fed up with yet another e-mail that pronounces yet another policy or procedure affecting the way you do things. Similarly, your role may be affected by changes in IT that will impact on the way you do your job, and by management's vision and ideas. But welcome change and embrace it: the company that stands still will soon be out of business or taken over by one of its competitors. Show you understand change: your boss will be busy with the strategy so do what you can to help with the implementation. Why not pull the support staff together and write a presentation for them that your boss can deliver explaining the changes?

Changes to management structures can provide plenty of opportunities for people to carve a new role for themselves and really show their worth. Study any pronouncements about the company's vision and the strategy for achieving that vision; then you'll be in a better position to contribute to it. Try to understand how any changes in the way this vision will be carried out may affect your organisation and in particular the way you work, and colleagues alongside you. Work out what you personally can do to contribute to the goals and to promote the vision and changes required to achieve them along the way. Discuss this with your boss to see how he or she (and therefore you) will be affected – the boss may have some ideas of what you can do.

Case study: Expect and welcome change
Kathy, PA, retail company

I've been with this company for 30 years, so have come to expect change and welcome it – I've certainly seen a lot of change in my time. The world has been changing ever since the year dot at a faster and faster rate, so why should it stop now? Our customers' needs and expectations are changing all the time, so our products are bound to change – when I started, you never had 24-hour openings, or the ability to move produce around so quickly. I greet change positively, although it can be a real nuisance at the time, as you get used to new systems, because I think it's a sign our company is moving forward with the times. There are benefits too. I'm hoping to take three months' leave shortly, as part of a new life-friendly perk our company has introduced. I think the important thing to do is to look after yourself when your company is going through huge change, because it is stressful. Put yourself in the place of those at the top: not only do they have to create a strategy which will fight off the competition, but they also have the lovely job of convincing everybody else – the employees – why such a change is necessary and worth any temporary disruption. There are political implications, as well – you should try to work out how it will affect your section and boss.

The other thing which is changing constantly is the new technological developments – they are having a major impact on the way in which business is done and companies operate. When I started, I was using an electronic typewriter. Now, it's all PC work and I've got my own projects, such as sitting on a committee to look at ways to improve staff benefits. Life is much more interesting and fun – and you feel as though you're putting far more in and getting much more out.

Case study: Expect change to the working day
Mario, PA to the legal director in an investment bank

One of the frustrating things about this job is that you can spend time planning and organising a day – only to find that everything changes because your boss has to travel at a moment's notice. The whole perfectly planned day can be blown by a phone call or an e-mail. So you have to be able to rearrange things very rapidly and also set up what the boss now needs and do it in such a way that everything happens very smoothly. If you're calling to say your boss can't make a meeting, you can't sound flustered and panicky, because it doesn't sound very professional. You can build up yourself, your boss and company a great credit rating by the way you handle such phone calls. Handling and reacting to change goes with the territory of the job – if you're the sort of person who always expects everything to go as you've set it up, then you're going to be disappointed. Business accepts that cancellations are part of life – it happens.

You can also get a sense of control by driving change yourself and challenging yourself to do things differently. You can offer new ways of working, solutions and ideas. Think them through before you present them – the downsides, the upsides, financial and team benefits. Take the initiative, contribute to your organisation's aims, recognise opportunities and develop strategies for converting them into action; and work cooperatively with others to achieve results. You'll raise your profile and give yourself far more control.

Having knowledge gives you a feeling of control. Find out what happened at meetings by asking questions – make a habit of it and your boss will start to realise you really want to know. Don't ask closed questions that just require a closed answer, such as 'Did the meeting go well?' Use the word 'How?', which suggests to people that you expect answers in words of more than one syllable. Ask, 'What happens next?' One of the main complaints from PAs is that their bosses never tell them anything – but that's partly because too many PAs don't ask enough questions.

Finally, when you get a new boss, go out of your way to help him, because the new boss will remember your support. Give the relationship time to work and don't compare your new boss unfavourably with your old one. He is bound to have different ideas of what a PA does, so sit down for a while to explain your role and discuss what is expected of you. Offer to relay any changes in working practices the boss will want to the team. A new boss could be a blessing, releasing any previous brakes on your career development. Of course, he could try to impose them...

Making use of your appraisal

Appraisals are important because they enable you to focus on what you've achieved, so boosting your confidence, and on the future and where you want to be. For that reason alone, it's worth doing one of your own, outside of work, every six months, so that you can work out whether the company you're with now is likely to feature in your life a couple of years down the road. Look to see how the appraisals can complement each other.

Even if your company doesn't operate an appraisal system, sit down with your boss(es) to discuss your role and your performance every six months or so. At interview, you should have had an opportunity to find out what your boss(es) expect of you. After the first month or so, review the parameters of your relationship. Six months into the role, as your skills and experience broaden and you get to know the organisation and how it functions and your niche in it becomes more defined, redefine your relationship and your role. Identify what's going particularly well, and then move to problem areas. If you're not expecting an easy ride, talk it through with somebody from human resources or someone you trust beforehand who can give you advice and pointers. Use the process to make your boss aware of the responsibilities you have and the way in which your role and your career have moved forward. Show how you've added value to the organisation, and then you are justified to ask for an increase in salary or training. Outline where you have strong and weak areas, and ask for training to strengthen them further or help you put them right.

Use the opportunity to suggest ways in which your boss can help you do a better job. It may be telling you where he is going rather than disappearing off for lunch without telling you, or stopping interrupting you when you're in the middle of something. Come up with some concrete examples of times when the boss has done wrong and he will recognise them. If you have a boss who doesn't handle people well, now's the time to talk about it. The boss may not realise the impact his behaviour has on the rest of the team.

If you feel that your career is moving forward, that's great. Watch where your job is going, so that you can steer it in the direction you want.

Case study: Your career is your responsibility

Annette, PA to a management consultant

Whatever they claim at interview, most organisations don't have a structured, planned training programme for secretaries. Don't wait for the annual review to ask for training if you feel you'd benefit from it sooner rather than later. In any case, I find often people have their annual review and point out what they want to do and get trained in, and then nothing happens. That's partly the PAs' fault – they don't take the initiative and follow it through. You can't expect bosses to sort your career out for you; they're far too busy doing other things and, anyway, what's relevant for your company now probably won't be in six months' time. If your copy of your appraisal with all your plans in it is still lying in your drawer after six months gathering dust, then that's your problem. Keep it out where you can see it and make it act as a reminder of the career path you want. It's your career; you must drive it forward.

Boost your knowledge

Root out information on your organisation and the sector. Aim to be the eyes and ears of a company. Sitting quietly and complaining that nobody ever tells you what is going on or how to do things won't improve matters or put you in a good light. The more you know about your organisation, the better a job you will be able to do. Ask questions, find things out and work out how things are done. Be proactive.

Know who the bosses are, so that, if they ring up to speak to you or anyone else, you can immediately identify them. Try to develop a memory for names and faces – saying people's names several times as you talk to them will help. When you see familiar faces, go up and ask how they are. They may not remember your name, so give them a hand: reintroduce yourself. Try to remember something you've found out about each person – it may be someone had just had a baby when you met last, or a holiday in France – anything that you can hook on to and ask about. People will be impressed that you remembered.

Do your homework – keep up to date and informed. Read widely about the sector. If you work for a corporate, follow its fortunes in the financial pages of the papers; check its Web site to see what's new. Expand your skills base to show you're interested in the sector. Read publications such as _Crème_ for Web sites that will help you do a better job faster and make a note of them; and check their Web sites and those such as www.pa-assist.com and www.fasttrack-digital.com to pick up tips and advice. They can tell you a lot about the business services available to individuals and orgaisations.

You can develop your own trade mark, something you're known for in your company, a particular skill nobody else has, which could be as simple as helping newcomers settle in, whatever their level, or something nobody else is as good at. Be an expert at what you enjoy doing the best. Show your mastery of software packages and the Internet – be the one everybody comes to in the office. Or be the expert at organising meetings and conferences, ensuring that everything goes just right. Be a great teacher and leader. Develop an expertise in choosing office equipment and ensuring it is maintained. Know how to handle information. If you can do this in just one area, you'll strengthen your chances of remaining employed when others are being made redundant.

Boost your confidence

It's easy to read self-help books and then forget about putting what they say into practice, or give it a go for a couple of weeks and lose enthusiasm and effort after that. There are courses at local colleges in the evenings and during weekends designed to improve important soft skills such as listening and handling people, and boosting your confidence. There is no substitute for doing and trying things out, especially if those around you clearly appreciate your efforts and say so; and if you can see people and organisations benefiting from your actions and ideas then you should be proud of that and add it to your CV. Keep a file of all the things you've done, and include people's comments on your performance and the job done, and the way you've handled difficult people or situations:

- Do checklists and tick things off as you go down them, so that you know you are getting things done.
- Enhance your learning abilities.
- Boost your memory.
- Keep track of things that went well and why, and what sort of role you played in them.
- Create the right image by using the right body language – don't slouch in front of your PC, for example.

- Learn how to state your needs effectively without fear of being a nuisance or being told no. Remember, effective PAs ask for what they need.
- Don't just limit the 'trying things out' to the office. Boost your confidence out of work and you'll see the effects in work, too.

Case study: Boost your confidence by doing and learning

Amanda, PA in media

It's important to learn how to handle aggressive and demanding people if you're going to be a top PA, and there are certainly more of them around, be they office bullies or clients. It's no coincidence that there are more courses on phone rage for front-line staff. Half the time these people hope that by being aggressive or rude they will scare you into helping them more than you should. The other half, it's just their way, and they aren't even aware that they are doing it.

You'll pick up a lot 'on the job', or through courses such as 'Handling Difficult People' or 'Conflict Resolution'. These may be put on in-house, or you can pick them up at adult education colleges or professional training organisations. Alternatively, take on voluntary projects at work. If you can think carefully about what you've handled well, and badly, in a day, then such active learning will help you develop ways to improve your skills in the future. You have to know how to handle conflict in terms of aggressive people, but also in terms of clients and customers (who comes first: Company A or Organisation B?).

So:

- Make a note of your achievements.
- Note your failures – what have you learnt from them?
- Work out where you want to go next – don't stay in the same place for long or you may get bored.

The next chapter will help you move on and upwards so that you can plot your career path.

Summary

▧ Aim to build consistently good performance and to get things right first time, every time.

▧ Break any projects down into small bits so that they become more manageable and, even if you have a busy day, you can fit one small bit in when you have time to do so.

▧ Keep learning something new every day.

▧ Try to do things faster and more cheaply.

▧ Set goals for yourself, not just at work but outside it. The way you feel about your achievements in your life will be evident to those around you.

▧ Learn from the colleagues you admire. What is it about their approach that makes them the success they are? Their passionate yet detached outlook? The way they prepare for something? Their image? The way they handle colleagues?

▧ Know your values and be prepared to change. What worked yesterday may not work tomorrow.

▧ Be results-oriented. Show what you have produced. Always aim to show an outcome.

10 Managing your further rise to the top

An integral part of career success is to know what you want and how you're going to get it and then to keep reviewing what you want. You may find that, as you move through life, your idea of your niche and what success means changes, so it's important to revisit your goals and aspirations just to check you're on track. Things can happen that determine these changes – you may meet that special person, who may move abroad and you may decide to relocate as well; you may get pregnant, or married, or both; you might get made redundant or be deeply affected by a personal event in your life, perhaps somebody dying or falling ill, or, more impersonally, by a major event such as the terrorist attack on the World Trade Center in September 2001, which makes you question your values and motives for working and living. In your 20s, you may feel quite happy to spend every hour given to you during the week to do your job, be it with clients in the evening or working on client presentations due the following day. Your 30s may see a change in that you start seeing your life go by – if you live to 90, that's a third of it gone, and you start to question what you're on earth for and what you want to achieve in life. Age can make us all more tolerant and eager to do things for the good of society and earth. You can get to the top in your 20s, and then something will happen and an event makes you refocus and re-evaluate your life and what you want out of it.

In a fast-changing world, it's important for each of us to know how to cope and keep up with change. If we can seize opportunities to take control, grow and develop where we see them, then we should run with them. The joy of the secretarial and PA role is that you will have plenty of chances to do just that – if you decide to take them. It certainly is an area where the more you choose to do, the more you can weight your role in a direction you want it to go in. You can then focus on what you want to do, as opposed to being made to do the stuff you don't.

Create change yourself – don't wait for it to take over your life

For all the fantastic opportunities a career as a PA offers, more than any other the secretarial world is one in which it is also possible to get very comfy in the same position for too long, without your career moving on. Although this may suit some people, it's important to remember that, although your career may stay static, the world around you won't. This is particularly important to remember if you find yourself in an organisation where it suits the management and structure of the company if the secretaries remain confined to their roles. After you've been in the job and got established in your role, and picked up company practices and procedures, and formed a solid working relationship with your boss, it's time to start thinking about pushing things on.

Be a rebel – push back boundaries

Don't feel you have to stick to the well-behaved approach. Be a rebel. Look for ways to develop a can-do philosophy – don't concentrate on what you *can't* do. Think about what you can. Don't stick too closely to rules or past systems – if they are getting in the way, come up with a new system or way of operating, so that past ways don't frustrate those trying to get their jobs done. And then make sure people know there is an alternative to sticking to the rules. Look for every opportunity you can to develop your skills *and boost your confidence*.

The more you stick to your job description, the more you're limiting your learning opportunities, so go out there, be a rebel and show what you can do. If there is no obvious PA ladder to climb, perhaps because you work for a small company, then offer to take on a particular responsibility and take ownership of it, even if it means doing it outside of your working hours at first. Look at your own company to see what you can take on in your own right to extend your portfolio of skills so that you can develop. Once you've got an idea in your head that you think you can pursue, then sell it to your bosses in terms of how that idea will benefit the organisation, not your career. Think 'team', think 'us' – your idea is more likely to be accepted. Think 'I', think 'my career goals', and your idea will lose power immediately because apparently it will benefit only one person – you. If management is your goal, start taking on any management jobs you can so that you get into the management way of thinking, doing and being. You could end up with a higher salary and new title, such as PA/project manager or PA/IT projects manager, like Marge in the following case study.

Case study: Find something you're good at and develop that skill
Marge, manages a team of secretaries in a legal firm

I look after a fee earner in the group, but he has partly retired, so I also lead a group of 20 secretaries and it's my job to make sure they all fit well with their teams. I give newcomers an induction and make sure all the technology is set up for them on their first day. I'm responsible for ensuring that we have sufficient permanent staff on so that we're not over-loaded with temporary staff, and choosing the agency we recruit staff from. I have really tried to develop a strong team approach this year and I've organised several social events to get people working together as a team, and had the training department in to deliver sessions on handling difficult people, IT packages and presentations. I also have to hand out work in the form of new assignments. I really enjoy being leader of the pack and helping people develop their roles and skills. I'm passionate about pulling everybody together and helping people make the most of their working lives.

In a role like this, team building, delegating, negotiating and motivating others are key elements of the job. I spend some of my time helping our HR team interview candidates and select new recruits; I know all the lawyers, their personalities and the way they work, so I could judge how well candidates would 'fit' in with them and the team. I appraise the team, disciplining staff and identifying training needs. Senior management rely on me to promote the positive side of change and ensure that my team can handle it.

Find out what courses are on offer, how much they will cost and how much time you'll need out of the office, and present them to your boss in terms of 'This is how I will be able to do my job more effectively as a result of doing this course.' The good manager should provide opportunities for you to develop your abilities, be they technological in nature or soft skills and managerial. Work out with your boss ways in which you can get things done more effectively and faster between you so you can build your skills by taking on new projects.

If you approach your boss and ask if you can go on a course, be very clear about what the outcome will be – 'If I go on the course, it will benefit the business because I will be able to...' Show how the company will reap rewards and then be explicit when you do things you learn on the course itself. It's proof it was worth going on, and that the company has invested wisely in training you.

Is your career developing at a sufficiently fast pace for you?

To ensure that you are moving your career forward, there are strategies you can develop such as rewriting your CV every six months. This will help you identify what you can add to it that is new in terms of your achievements, skills and experience (both in and out of work) and what you would *want* to add to it in the six months ahead and, say, two years hence. In this way, you can ensure that you look for opportunities that will enable you to plot your career path.

Many PAs have moved up the ladder into management, marketing, training, human resources, information technology and administration. For the most part, they have had to make the push themselves. Many companies and bosses simply don't know how to make the most of their employees, perhaps because they don't have the time to do it, even if they claim that 'People are the most important resource.' Don't get stuck in a rut: if your boss seems reluctant to discuss your next step, take action yourself. Ultimately, of course, this may mean changing companies – or starting up on your own. The key is that you take the action required to move your career forward to where you want it to be. If nothing is happening where you are, then you owe it to yourself to take charge and change all that.

Case study: If things aren't working out, move on
Darren, PA in an executive search company to two directors

I joined an executive search company as a secretary on the basis that they promised I could get into researching a particular sector to get into sourcing and finding candidates. After six months, nothing had happened and I was still in the same position. I realised nothing was going to change, so signed up with a couple of recruitment agencies. Two months later, I left to join another search company in the City. It was an immediate 50 per cent PA, 50 per cent research role. If I hadn't made the move, I would still be typing letters now. If things aren't going the way you expected, you have to get out there and do something about it. The first company I joined – well, it suited them to have a typist and they weren't going to change a thing. At least I learnt how executive search companies function, which was useful for my second role. I wish I'd had the chance to talk to other PAs at the interview stage to find out how many had moved up the ladder.

Alternatively, this may mean taking on a project that becomes exclusively yours, so that you develop a niche for yourself that expands your job and gives you something to do in your own right.

Drive your own career to where you want it to go

Experience on the job enables you to build up self-management skills: effective networking; being able to persuade and influence other people; managing yourself and your workload; and your interpersonal skills. Most PAs will be able to fine-tune these with experience over the years.

It also enables you to build up job-specific skills, such as human resource management, training new and existing staff, IT, using e-mail and the Internet. These will require more drive to achieve, because you will need to make the push that ensures you acquire them. Although they may start out as short-term projects, you will need to look for ways to make these long term. You don't want those projects that use such skills to disappear after getting them off the ground – seek to build on them.

Ask for more responsibility or pinpoint areas that interest you, and you're more likely to end up with projects you enjoy that could lead to promotion. If you don't, you're more likely to be landed with the lousy jobs that nobody wants. Figure 10.1 sets out an approach to driving your career to where you want it to go.

As you work your way up the career ladder, consider which way you want to drive your career. Do you want to:

▦ work for more senior people as a PA, eventually to be the PA to a chairman or chief executive of a major company, either through being promoted up through the PA ladder within one company or moving from one to another every two or three years, as you gain more seniority and experience?
▦ expand your role so that you are part PA, part project manager?
▦ have tremendous autonomy and be able to impact totally on the organisation, for example by being office manager or the linchpin who pulls everybody together as the only PA?

150

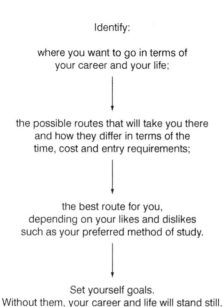

Identify:

where you want to go in terms of
your career and your life;

the possible routes that will take you there
and how they differ in terms of the
time, cost and entry requirements;

the best route for you,
depending on your likes and dislikes
such as your preferred method of study.

Set yourself goals.
Without them, your career and life will stand still.

Figure 10.1 Driving your career

▓ move into a new role using new-found skills, such as recruiting, training, marketing, managing or information technology?

Working for more senior people, you may need experience in a particular sector – 'Three years working in property required.' Alternatively, you may need to have worked for a certain number of years at a specific level – 'Board experience a must' – or for a certain type of company – 'Experience of working for a FTSE company essential', so you are used to knowing how these companies work. Some organisations require a specific skill, depending on the role they have in mind – 'Previous start-up experience vital.' At this level, the emphasis will be on your brainpower and the standard of your work, as opposed to typing speeds.

There are different ways to move on and up:

▓ by chance – simply meeting the boss, who happens to be looking for a PA anyway, and just hitting it off, and the boss then saying, 'Will you come and work for me?';

▌ by working for large corporates and working your way up until you are working for the very highest levels of management, either for the same boss or leapfrogging from one to another; and doing stints of covering for more senior PAs while they are on holiday or off sick – 'I can hold the fort, don't worry' – you know it won't be for long;

▌ working for a small company in which you are the linchpin who holds it all together with an office manager/PA sort of role;

▌ your boss moving to another position (not necessarily with the same company) and you moving with the boss;

▌ your employer deciding to restructure the organisation, which changes your role, giving you a chance to break out;

▌ working for an entrepreneur or family;

▌ networking carefully with those who will introduce you to the right people.

Chasing promotion

Career development can be a matter of luck, and being in the right place at the right time, but it can also be a result of looking forward and planning, actively seeking to boost skills, experience and planned networking. Establish a network of contacts within your company, including the human resources department, and outside it.

If you want to go on up the ladder, it is important that you know what is happening across your organisation. Get to know who is who amongst the secretaries and who works for the top people. Offer to look after those more senior to you while their secretaries are on holiday, not because you are hoping to boot them out of a job but because it will give you the chance to find out what life is like in a more senior role for a short – and manageable – period of time, and to show you whether one day it might be for you. Learn from those who look after a more senior person, from the way they dress and present themselves to the way they handle people.

Let it be known at your appraisal that you want to go on up the ladder, and check to see if you can expand your skills set to narrow any gaps in your knowledge. Talk to human resources about other opportunities that will enable you to move on up the ladder, so that they can have your name on a list of possible candidates.

Finally, if you want to be promoted, don't disappear at the dot of 5 o'clock. Always stay late to go the extra mile. If you're interested in what's going on, then you will always be able to find a way to contribute and add something extra.

Raise your profile and increase the power of your network

You can also buy yourself time if you sharpen your focus and know exactly where your career is heading. At the same time, you want to acquire a reputation for being seriously good at what you are doing, and head and shoulders above the rest, for you never know where this might lead. Try to create win/win situations and try to develop long-standing working relationships. Talk with enthusiasm about what you're doing and those you work with. Tell people whom you're working for and what you're doing, especially if you've worked for a similar team or person(s) at a similar level. Find out what they do. If you can find a way to develop the relationship, such as doing lunch, helping them out, recognising them when they call, asking about the weekend in Venice they mentioned they were doing – then do it.

Try to get involved on a project or committee that works across your organisation, so that you get to know people in different sections and teams. You could be on a social committee, a charitable committee, or a group that initiates a policy on the use of the Internet or comments on the travel company your firm uses; perhaps you can be the support staff rep – anything that will raise your name in your own right. Volunteer to do anything that will bring you into contact with those at the top – do an interview with them for the company newsletter, or put their career profile on the Web site. Think of things that will get you noticed and give you clout. If you can do this in an area you want to get involved in, it will help you get a foothold in it.

Establish a reputation as an expert in something – perhaps IT, or your local knowledge of restaurants and hotels that are suitable for events and dinners. It could be people within the company or a particular knowledge of where you can find something out that brings people to your door saying, 'I've been told you're the person to ask, because you're the fountain of knowledge in this place.' Use opportunities such as these as a way to raise your profile and prove your effectiveness in handling people, solving problems and thinking of the team. This is where it can be very useful to answer the phone. Even taking messages gives you a chance to raise your profile and imprint your name on somebody else's mind, if you handle the call 100 per cent professionally.

Finally, it's important to be aware that moving up may involve moving on, as well. Keep up to date with the recruitment market and methods of hiring, and fine-tune your CV every six months. If you think you're going to hit a ceiling within your company, try to meet other PAs elsewhere. Remember that your experience can be very useful to other sectors; for example, legal secretaries may move into investment banking, and conference organisers can move into the hotel sector or banking sector.

Secretarial events, such as the larger conventions (like the Times Crème Executive Secretarial and PA Exhibition, held in May), give you a chance to keep in touch with what is going on and to network with people who may be able to help you. They have lots of seminars – as do most careers events – on planning your career, moving forward, getting further qualifications and boosting your skills to do a good job. Web sites such as pa-assist.com and www.fasttrack-digital.com enable you to network; and you should stay in touch with agencies and recruitment consultants who've helped you in your career, so that they can keep you in mind for positions as they come in.

Broaden your role and acquire new skills

If you want to go on up the career ladder, it will be important to keep up to date with technical, managerial and social skills and you should identify all the training that is available to you, both in-house and out of the workplace.

Build up a base of skills in an area that interests you and that you know you're good at. The Accreditation of Prior Learning system with a local college may mean you can fast-track qualifications, such as National Vocational Qualifications. Some of these are designed for those who are new to the supervisory role, and they are practical in nature. Qualifications indicate your level of competency and show you're committed to your chosen career. You can acquire qualifications in areas such as:

- management (Diploma in Management);
- supervisory management;
- marketing (Certificate in Marketing);
- personnel practice;
- training practice (Chartered Institute of Personnel and Development certificate);
- administrative management;
- international trade and services;
- school administration;
- information technology.

Some of the professional bodies are listed in Chapter 11, 'Useful addresses'. They offer different levels of courses, from the first-step course for those who are just starting out in an area, such as training, to courses for those who are actively employed in the area and want to acquire qualifications to prove their competence and commitment to the field.

You can develop new skills by taking on new projects or attending courses. There are courses, for example, for those who've just been landed with the role of supervising other people. You can study for whole certificates or diplomas, covering subjects such as managing people, managing information, managing resources and managing activities. Don't wait for the company to identify your training needs – suggest them yourself. If necessary, train in your own time and take out a career development loan – view your training as an investment. All too often, secretaries and PAs are expected to learn by osmosis and little is actually done to boost their training and skills base, especially in the soft skills side. Talented people make their careers happen. They drive them. Make lifelong learning a feature from cradle to grave.

Some secretarial Web sites will give you pointers as to useful courses you can do, and the advice and tips columns are also useful. Management books may inspire you as you read how others have risen through the ranks. Each of us has a preferred learning style: some swear by doing, others by taking a course at an adult education college with a human being to guide and teach us, and others are happy to log in online and suss the whole thing with the aid from the tutor by e-mail.

Check out the Web site www.lifelonglearning.co.uk and also visit the Industrial Society Learning and Development Web site, as it runs many training courses for secretaries and PAs – go to www.is learning.co.uk. Some of their courses for secretaries and PAs include:

- the secretarial role;
- writing and minute taking;
- building a better partnership for managers and PAs;
- working with others;
- building confidence;
- business writing skills.

Usefully, they run courses called 'The Executive Secretary/PA in Management Today' and 'How to Be Happy with Change'.

But they also have others on communication and leadership skills, including conflict resolution skills, emotional intelligence (advancing your interpersonal skills), the manager as a skilful communicator and confidence at work (transforming performance by building esteem). And that includes courses for frontline staff (including one on phone rage), and on time for your life (managing home and work, and time for the team – managing your team's time and productivity).

Asking for a pay increase

If you feel it's time you had a pay hike and decide to go for it, plot your case with care. Find out what other PAs at your level (bearing in mind your experience) and in your sector are being paid. You can find this out by looking at the recruitment pages in publications such as *Crème*, checking salary levels on Web pages such as www.reed.co.uk, talking to recruitment agency staff who should know what the going rate is for somebody with your experience, and talking to individuals (although many people are reluctant to divulge their salary levels).

Next, work out *why* you feel you deserve a rise. Relate your skills to results. Pinpoint all your achievements since your last increase and since you've joined the firm; note down any added value contributions you've made, or extra responsibilities you've volunteered for. Note any cost-cutting options you've suggested that have been implemented; in other words, go prepared and armed.

Set a time aside when you and your boss(es) can discuss this issue face to face in privacy, a time when you are not under pressure, and once in the meeting state your case clearly, assertively and professionally. Do not discuss these things by e-mail, a cowardly way out in a situation in which you're supposed to be proving your worth. A number of things may happen: your request may be rejected out of hand, in which case you should be given reasons why; your boss(es) may take note of your request, and tell you they will have to come back to you after thought and consideration; or (unlikely) it may be approved on the spot, in which case you should go out and buy yourself a bottle of champagne. This third option is only likely if you've given your boss an indication of what the meeting is about and he or she has had an opportunity to check with the appropriate channels and review the situation.

If you are not given a pay rise, you have a number of ways to move forward. You could see what happens in six months' time, or when the next overall review of salaries takes place, or after your review has been held. You could find another position. Whatever you decide, you've taken a step forward in asking for a rise – it takes nerve and shows that you've got self-esteem and confidence in your own abilities.

It's best not to resign because you don't get a pay rise, unless you really work for a pittance. Think things through. If you really do have to resign, make sure your boss hears it from you first.

Manage your stress

Being a top PA is stressful, if you care about what you're doing, and the hours can be long. You're supporting everybody else – but who supports you? You probably go home at the end of a day, picking up some milk at the corner shop if it's still open, cook dinner, talk to the kids and/or the cat, open your mail. Who is supporting you in your life?

You know how much stress you're under and, if you're informed about the symptoms of stress, you can pinpoint them and then dictate that it's time to slow down. Some stress is good for us – it provides the adrenalin we need to do that extra-brilliant job. But that's not always the case, especially if you don't have the most supportive of bosses. Ways to manage stress include:

- Recognise you are stressed.
- Give yourself an extra-early start in the day to do tasks that you can do alone – and then go out and treat yourself to a coffee or pain au chocolat.
- Make it easier to find things on your desk – get organised. Find a system that suits you – you may need a couple of them.
- Create a work area that pleases your eye and nose – get flowers in every week.
- Don't deliberately work long hours just for the sake of it. Get a couple of days a week when you leave bang on time.
- See yourself as somebody worth spoiling. Treat yourself to the things that make you feel special.
- Find something to do on a daily basis that you enjoy. It could be playing the guitar, reading poetry, cooking – anything that takes your mind away from the office.

Moving up where you are: what's stopping you?

If people aren't getting to where they want to be, it's because:

- They don't know where that is, or haven't given it serious thought.
- They lack the time (ie the commitment to make the change).
- They lack the money (so budget for it and cut out other things).
- They fear making a change – what will everybody say? (Never mind them, it's your life!)
- They believe that they 'can't do anything else, I've done this for so long'.
- They just think, 'It's easier to stay where I am' – but for how much longer?
- The opportunity just isn't there.

Plan ways around these points and tackle them. If you really want
to do something, you'll find a way. Never underestimate the skills
you have under your belt as a good PA. You probably know more
about people and information technology than most people in
your organisation, for starters.

'My boss is so awful to me, and says I'm so useless that I'd never get another job, anyway. What would I do for a reference?'

If you've got a boss who resembles Attila the Hun – and let's face
it, they do exist, however charming they pretended to be when
you went for your interview – the chances are that other people
notice how awful he is to you and will think you handle him bril-
liantly. Find out how many other secretaries the boss has gone
through so that you know it's not just you. Of course, your boss
might be so stressed as not even to realise the effect his behaviour
and expectations are having on you. Put aside some time to
discuss them. And if your boss won't make time or change, plan
your exit. At the end of the day, we spend too many hours at work
to put up with bullies. If things go out of control, and you get fired,
visit www.justgotsacked.com, which gives advice on employment
problems resulting from dismissal or potential dismissal. It will
help your case if you can:

- Keep a diary of instances where a boss has been foul, especially
  if other people were in earshot. When complaining you must
  use facts, not opinions.
- Show yourself to be a professional to as many people as you
  can.
- Raise your profile in other departments, by sitting in on an
  extra committee and taking minutes at meetings. Other people
  will notice your abilities and enthusiasm and will sit up and
  take note, making a transfer to another section easier.
- Get involved outside the office and use your skills, for example
  taking minutes at meetings, so that other people can act as
  referees too if you move to another organisation altogether.
- Use temping to secure yourself a new job – you can start
  proving yourself from the first hour.

Most bosses are fairly human, and recognise their employees' will to move on and go places with their careers; as you give in your notice, you can always raise their egos by thanking them for all the opportunities they've given you over the years to develop your skills and saying what brilliant bosses they were.

Leaving the secretarial role behind: can it be done?

PAs will remain employed so long as they continue to upgrade their skills, both once they've found a PA position and before they start to look. They need to be on the lookout for opportunities to move with the flow of change in terms of how their organisation conducts itself and its business *and* in terms of how the workplace is changing. The winners in the years ahead will be those who have a sharp eye on the job marketplace and give some time to thinking seriously about where they are going. The losers will be those who expect others to plan their jobs and careers for them.

You'll know when it's time to move on, so do something about it. The reality is that your boss will be too busy focusing on survival to make things happen for you – and you may not want the boss to know your career plans, anyway, if they mean moving away from the firm. So:

- Work out what success means to you – what are you hungry for?
- Develop a plan for achieving that success.
- Acquire any extra skills or knowledge you'll need to achieve it.
- Take responsibility for your own learning.
- Create your own path – it's your career, nobody else's.

Summary

- Balance your career goals up against your life goals, that is, what you want to achieve in work and outside it.

▤ PAs have a tremendous ability to transfer skills across from one career to another, more so than in any other career. PAs have greater flexibility in the job market than any other group, particularly if they market themselves skilfully.

▤ So set yourself goals, and you're more likely to get to where you want to be. Goals can be set in any area of life, but they should be SMART:
  - **S**pecific;
  - **M**easurable;
  - **A**chievable;
  - **R**elevant;
  - **T**ime-Based.

▤ Remember that what matters most is that, at the end of the day, you have the top job for _you_!

11 *Useful addresses*

Institute of Qualified Private Secretaries
First Floor, 6 Bridge Avenue, Maidenhead SL6 1RR.
Tel: (01628) 625007; Fax: (01628) 624990; www.iqps.org
A professional organisation for career-minded secretaries, PAs and lecturers in business studies. You will receive invitations to local and national conferences, receive the quarterly magazine, *Career Secretary*, and, importantly, be able to show that you consider yourself to be a professional. You'll also have access to IQPS video training and overseas contacts, as well as information about secretarial exhibitions.

www.fasttrack-digital.com
A Web site offering lots of online and CD ROM training courses in a wide variety of subjects. Currently, there are 5,000 members of Fasttrack, all of whom benefit from the opportunity to network with each other, train and acquire careers advice. Fasttrack also has a magazine, and runs seminars and events.

Recruitment and Employment Confederation
36–38 Mortimer Street, London W1W 7RG. Tel: (020) 7462 3260; www.rec.uk.com
The professional body for individuals and companies involved in recruitment.

The following professional bodies can provide useful careers information and details pertaining to courses available if you wish to expand your skills base to focus on these areas:

Advertising Association
Abford House, 15 Wilton Road, London SW1V 1NJ. Tel: (020) 7828 2771; www.adassoc.org.uk

162

Association for Conferences and Events
ACE International, Riverside House, High Street, Huntingdon, Cambridgeshire PE29 3SG. Tel: (01480) 457595; www.martex. co.uk/ace

British Computer Society
1 Sanford Street, Swindon SN1 1HR. Tel: (01793) 417417; www. bcs.org.uk

Chartered Institute of Marketing
Moor Hall, Cookham, Maidenhead, Berkshire SL6 9QH. Tel: (01628) 427500; www.cim.co.uk

Chartered Institute of Personnel and Development
CIPD House, Camp Road, London SW19 4UX. Tel: (020) 8971 9000; www.cipd.co.uk

Chartered Management Institute
2 Savoy Court, Strand, London WC2R 0EZ. Tel: (020) 7497 0580; www.managers.org.uk

Institute of Administrative Management
40 Chatsworth Parade, Petts Wood, Orpington, Kent BR5 1RW. Tel: (020) 7612 7099; www.electranet.com.iam

Institute of Chartered Secretaries and Administrators (ICSA)
16 Park Crescent, London W1N 4AH. Tel: (020) 7580 4741; www.icsa.org.uk

Institute of Public Relations
The Old Trading House, 15 Northburgh Street, London EC1V 0PR. Tel: (020) 7253 5151; www.ipr.org.uk

Institute of Translation and Interpreting
Exchange House, 494 Midsummer Boulevard, Central Milton Keynes MK9 2EA. Tel: (01908) 255905; www.iti.org.uk

Society for Editors and Proofreaders
Riverbank House, 1 Putney Bridge Approach, London SW6 3JD. Tel: (020) 7736 3278; www.sfep.org.uk

12 *Further reading*

Job hunting

Cornfield, Rebecca (1999) *Successful Interview Skills*, 2nd edn, Kogan Page, London

Golzen, G and Kogan, H (1999) *The Daily Telegraph Guide to Working for Yourself*, Kogan Page, London

Greenwood, David (2000) *Job Hunters Handbook*, Kogan Page, London

Krechowiechka, Irene (2000) *Net that Job!*, Kogan Page, London

Yate, Martin John (2001) *Great Answers to Tough Interview Questions*, Kogan Page, London

Yate, Martin and Dourlain, Terra (2001) *Online Job Hunting: Great answers to tough questions*, Kogan Page, London

Working abroad

Golzen, G and Kogan, H (2000) *The Daily Telegraph Guide to Working Abroad*, 22nd edn, Kogan Page, London

Griffith, Susan (2001) *Work Your Way Round the World*, Vacation Work Publications

Living and Working in... series, How To Books, Oxford

Working for yourself

Capstick, Anthony B (1998) *How to Change Your Life with Technology: Start your own business with just a computer and a phone link*, Management Books 2000, Chalford, Gloucestershire

Goleman, Daniel (1996) *Emotional Intelligence*, Bloomsbury, London

Jeffries, Susan (1987) *Feel the Fear and Do It Anyway*, Arrow, London

Index